Busy Life, Peaceful Center

Busy Life, Peaceful Center

A Book of Meditating

by Padraic O'Hare

ThomasMore
A DIVISION OF TABOR PUBLISHING
Allen, Texas • Chicago, Illinois

Send all inquiries to:
Thomas More Publishing
200 East Bethany Drive
Allen, Texas 75002–3804

Printed in the United States of America

ISBN 0–88347–291–0

1 2 3 4 5 99 98 97 96 95

CONTENTS

Acknowledgments

The wise person, in a path of faithfulness other than Christian, to whom I owe a special debt, as the reader will see, is Ven. Thich Nhat Hanh, Thay, teacher. The simplicity, clarity and profundity of the contemplative and compassionate insights embodied in his writing and in his life are much in evidence in these pages.

Thanks go, as well, to the colleagues at Merrimack College who served on the 1993/94 Faculty Development Committee for recommending the support of research for this book.

There is a legion of persons, at once deeply meditative and vigorously active, known to me personally or through the story of their lives as well as their writings, who quietly inspire whatever is inspired in these pages. Among these are Gustavo Gutierrez, David Ison, Laura Sperasi, Joan Chittister, Thomas Del Prete, Michael Moran, Gabriel Moran, Louise Cochran and, in the second category, William Shannon for his remarkable work with the wisdom of Thomas Merton, Abraham J. Heschel, Dorothy Day and, of course, "Father Louie" himself.

Some of the students who have participated in a course whose development accompanied the development of this book have been especially helpful. Among these are Claudia Marsh, Joan Rossi, Glenn Kealy, Bill Steele, Edith Roth, Thayer (Ted) Warshaw and a professorial colleague, John Dalphin.

Thanks to Gail Farmer for bringing her care and expertise to the development of the manuscript.

Special gratitude is extended to William "Doc" Miller for the encouragement of his words and the validation in his practice. Finally, I express love and gratitude for Peggy and Brian O'Hare. We share the busy life and they cope with my failures at the center.

DEDICATION

With Gratitude and Affection for:

Maria Harris

"The first Moment in teaching . . . is contemplation . . . to begin the teaching activity by seeing what is there. Thus we do not begin by preparing our material, we begin by being still. In this moment we are asked to see teaching as a Thou, so that we might bring to it an attitude of silence, reverence and respect."

Murray Rothman

"No," said the Rabbi, "these are not the ways you know that the night darkness is ended and the morning light has dawned. But, when you look into the eyes of another woman or man and see there not a stranger, but your brother or sister, then, no matter what time it is, the night darkness is broken and the light shines through."

The fact is that the mystical feeling of enlargement, union and emancipation has no specific intellectual content whatever of its own. It is capable of forming matrimonial alliances with material furnished by the most diverse philosophies and theologies, provided only that they can find a place in their framework for its peculiar emotional moods.

William James

Foreword

Foreword

One of my friends recently resigned from directing religious education in a large city church in order to give herself a six-month sabbatical. When she called me to talk about it I asked, "What moved you to the decision? Had you been thinking about it for a long while?"

Her answer came quickly. "I didn't realize I was, Marie, but I guess the dream was just under the surface." Then she continued. "It finally emerged one afternoon while I was sitting with a group of colleagues talking about people who'd influenced us spiritually. Someone said that her spirituality had been changed forever by a man she once dated—a man who was a farmer."

"She was a city person like me," my friend went on, "and she said that what she remembered most about him was his utter conviction that periodically, you have to let the land lie fallow. The moment I heard her say that, something happened inside me. I knew then that I had to do that too; I had to let the land of my own life, my own spirit, my own work lie fallow so that I might become who I'm called to be."

Padraic O'Hare's latest book, *Busy Life, Peaceful Center: A Book of Meditating* offers its readers the opportunity to let the land lie fallow. Like *The Way of Faithfulness,* his previous, award-winning book, it fosters our becoming centered people, contemplative people, holy people. Although most of us aren't able to resign from our jobs to take six months off, we are able to cultivate modes of being that enable us to live every day from the peaceful center that is ours if we cultivate it, and allow the land of our own being to be still in the midst of busyness. Ways exist for each of us to be genuine listeners to both the sounds and silences of a frequently noisy world.

But to learn these ways we often need the help of a guide, a master, a guru—and in his previous writing and his teaching, O'Hare has already proven himself unaffectedly capable of playing those roles. Here, he demonstrates this facility even further.

First he gives us a strong theological grounding for the meditation that is the focus of this book. He uses his own experience, but he also draws on the reflective heritage of other masters and other traditions—Merton, Gutierrez, Heschel, Hildegard, Thich Nhat Hahn and the two Johnsons: Elizabeth and William. He draws strongly on Judaism and Buddhism. As he does, he puts us in touch with a Holy One who is, in Hildegaard's words, "the breeze that nurtures all things; the rain coming from the dew causing the grass to laugh with the joy of life."

Second, he gives us a framework, an artistic form, for all of the meditative exercises he suggests to us, and show us how the form can become a habit. He tells us how to sit and how to stand, how to breathe and how to listen, how to start and how to finish our meditative practice—and when. He suggests music, and mantras, prayers, gathas and wise sayings so that we can give up the often diabolic temptation to be in charge of everything.

But most of all he does—in the writing and in the teachings of this book—what he is talking about. In other words, the book embodies what it points to, weds substance and form, so that as you read, you find yourself slowing down, becoming peaceful, and moving toward your own center. You find yourself lying fallow, awaiting whatever "word demanding and answer" (the phrase is Buber's) that may happen to you during your periods of genuine meditation.

I think this is the result of the author's powerful, unobtrusive style. Style is sometimes a trivialized term—especially for those to whom it suggest something ephemeral and not quite solid. But in artistry as well as in prayer, genuine style is essential: it's the way something is said, or done, or expressed, or performed; it's the combination of distinctive features of literary or artistic expression that—because they present a reality to us in a particular way—help us to see and to hear what we might not have noticed had the presentation been lacking in style. Here style is the shape of substance.

Reading the manuscript, I found the book's substance and style inseparable. Intertwined, they enriched my own spirituality in several ways, as they will enrich the readers' spiritualities in ways personal to them. In my case, they broadened my sensitivity to other religious traditions, even as I continued to cherish my own—reminding me the world's great religions need not be antagonists. The book's substance and style met me where I am—in the midst of life, with what seems like too many days when there is never enough time. They took my personal location seriously. I felt myself, as reader and as practitioner, treated with reverence and respect. And all along I was supported by the author's gentle irony, unobtrusive wit, and holy humor as once more I relearned I am not the center of the universe. Instead, we all are—we who are Chosen People, ludicrously yet lovingly placed at the heart of Creation by One who calls us to befriend and to dress that creation and to cherish one another and ourselves—in stillness, in solitude, and with an attitude of care that inevitably appears whenever we let the land lie fallow.

Maria Harris, author of *Dance of the Spirit*
and of *Jubilee Time* (Bantam)

Introduction

Introduction

I was conducting a course entitled "Contemplation and Compassion: Comparative Religious Perspectives" at Merrimack College in the summer of 1994. It was the second class of the course, one in which the focus is primarily on the practice of meditation and secondarily on study and conversation about the mystical, meditative or contemplative dimension of certain of the world's religions. We had just completed a half-hour period of seated meditation in a fashion adapted from Soto Zen Mindfulness meditation. The meditation was guided.

When, after a break to put the seminar room back in shape for conversation, we resumed class, a thoughtful adult student, musing on how pleasurable and refreshing the experience had been, said, "If only life were that simple."

Of course, if life were simple, there would be no meditation; the species simply would not have developed the practice of centering, composing, letting go, being still and emptying the interior self of irritation, distraction, fear, anxiety and toxins such as the seven deadly sins. It is because life is complex that some, sadly few and not triumphal about it, awaken to the need to be serious (not solemn) about the kind of self they are cultivating, the kind of masterpiece or wreck they are sculpting, moment by moment, and turn to the practice of being peaceful.

One of the classic expressions of the human state of complexity was spoken by Saint Paul when he said that what he willed he did not do. Complex indeed. Within a broad range of normalcy, excluding sociopaths, human beings wish to be kind and often are not. James Q. Wilson maintains that there is a natural human mechanism which he designates as "sympathy."[1] However, we will to be sympathetic and are not. The traditions of meditative or contemplative practice link human cruelty, small and great cruelties, to the toxins within, again the seven deadly sins or, in Buddhism, the "samyojana," the knots of forgetfulness of being. It is to share what simplicity and kindness I have found and practice as a result of practicing meditative prayerfulness that I offer this book.

The ideas about practice of meditative prayerfulness and the practices proposed here emerge from an interreligious mix; for I am persuaded, in the words of Diana Eck, that "if you understand only one religion, you don't understand any."[2] Here there is a certain challenge for some readers. The challenge grows exponentially, precisely in relationship to the depth of loyalty one has to a particular religious path and to the embodiment of clues to spiritual potentialities encased in an institutionalized religion. Some fear "false religion" when invited to meditate using physical and mental disciplines drawn from Zen Buddhism or fervent religious poetry of the Sufis. Therefore, the second reason for offering this book is to share the wondrous experience of being enriched and confirmed in one's path of holiness, as guided within one's own religious tradition, by the richness of insight and practice derived from other paths. Here the great model is Rabbi Heschel. During the deliberations of the Second Vatican Council in the mid 1960s, Rabbi Heschel worked with Vatican leaders, notably Cardinal Augustine Bea, to help frame the Council document which dealt with the Church's relations with the Jews. When even a late draft of what became the document, *Nostra Aetate,* still contained reference to a "mission to the Jews," Heschel changed his mode of dealing with some within the Vatican and announced publicly, with reference to the pernicious notion of a mission to the Jews, that he "would rather go to Auschwitz than give up my religion." Several years later, in 1972, not too long before his death, however, Rabbi Heschel responded to a question about the multiplicity of religious traditions by saying that it seemed to him "that religious pluralism is the will of God . . . that God is not a monopolist."[3]

What remarkable spiritual work Heschel must have engaged in during his lifetime, work of framing a masterpiece of faithfulness, to be able to be at once passionately Jewish and passionately reverential of all peoples.

To achieve some small semblance in our lives of what Rabbi Heschel achieved, we must be able to say, as Gabriel Moran wrote several years ago, that whereas Revelation may have a church and a synagogue and a mosque, and so on, the church does not have the Revelation.[4]

The organization of this book is threefold. Chapter one is a theological essay on the tension between being "in" a "religion" and being on a path of faithfulness. Chapter two is an essay on meditative practice. Chapter three is a series of ten guided meditation practice sessions.

Chapter One

Faithfulness and "Religion": Theological Reflections on Meditating

Faithfulness and Religion

There are two reasons for beginning a book "of meditating," which is to say a practical book—a book of practice—with a theological essay. The first reason is to respond to criticism of renewed interest in the meditative, the esoteric (as contrasted with the exoteric or external) features of religiousness. This criticism is especially sharp when directed at those raised in the West as Christians who show interest in Eastern practices. Such interest is seen as a fad and an escape, a dangerous expression of syncretism.

The second reason for beginning a book of meditative practice with a theological essay is to argue that the recovery of the meditative, or contemplative, heart of every path of faithfulness is the most radical corrective for what Max Weber called the "routinization" of religion. Far from being a danger, prizing the meditative or contemplative dimension of a path of faithfulness hastens the reform of religion.

It is certainly not a fad when Western Christians, for example, derive religious and theological inspiration from what Robley Whitson called "the coming convergence of world religions." In the Vatican Council II document *Ad Gentes*, the Council Fathers write, "Christians must learn to assimilate the ascetical and contemplative traditions planted by God in ancient cultures prior to the preaching of the Gospels."[1] Even more fullheartedly, without the touch of supersessionism that might be implied in the Councilar statement, the Sufi Master, Ibn Arabi, exclaims,

> My heart has become capable of every form:
> It is a pasture of gazelles,
> And a monastery for Christian monks,
> And a temple for idols,
> And the pilgrim's Ka'ba,
> And the tablets of the Torah,
> And the Book of the Qur'an.
> I follow the religion of love:
> Whatever way Love's camel takes,
> That is my religion and my faith.[2]

And the Trappist Master Thomas Keating writes, "The contemplative dimension of life, present in all the great religions, is the common heart of the world. There the human family is already one."[3]

It is equally without merit to characterize renewed interest in the practice of meditation, contemplation and prayer of silence as escape, a flight from the ethical focus of Liberal Protestantism and Conciliar Catholicism. The lives of the saints, Eastern and Western, ancient and contemporary, should be enough to convince thoughtful people that the true contemplative is always compassionate. As James Douglas, the evangelical Protestant social activist, has written in his book *Resistance and Contemplation*:

> If resistance is the yang of liberation, then contemplation is the yin . . . . If we wish to pass into the living truth of Jesus or Ghandi, we must affirm, as they did, the way of liberation as neither the yang of resistance nor the yin of contemplation but rather the one indivisible way . . . . As resistance seeks to liberate men and women from the pain of social injustice, contemplation seeks to liberate us from the pain of a yet deeper alienation: the impoverished and autonomous self.[4]

In a more positive key, a thoughtful theological assessment of the present interest in meditation and meditative prayerfulness reveals the link between this movement and the reform of religion itself.

"Religion" is everywhere, at all times and in all its particulars, in need of reformation. The famous distinction of Barth's comes to mind: that Christianity is not a religion at all, but a faith. By this

Barth meant that the very act of constructing religious institutions mires Christians in the idolatry of triumphalism, an overestimation of the importance of church structures and power relations. One need not agree with all that Barth meant by the distinction to appreciate that every feature of religion is in danger of losing vitality, of turning demonic, unless rendered vivid by real "faithfulness," which is to say by a deep loyalty to the Holy One expressed in action. It is for this reason that the great Rabbi Heschel wrote:

> Religion as an institution, the Temple as an ultimate end, or, in other words, religion for religion's sake, is idolatry. The fact is that evil is integral to religion, not only to secularism. Parochial saintliness may be an evasion of duty, an accommodation of selfishness. Religion is for God's sake. The human side of religion, its creeds, rituals and instructions, is a way rather than a goal. The goal is "to do justice, to love mercy and to walk humbly with thy God." When the human side of religion becomes a goal, injustice becomes a way.[5]

Consider that every feature of religion is subject to corruption: (1) the original *charismatic* enthusiasm gives way to "Cultural Christianity," exclusively cultural, as distinct from spiritual, reasons for belonging to a religion; (2) the *community* is everywhere in danger of being bureaucratized; (3) the *canon*, writings accepted as inspired, is turned into a dead letter in the hands of anxious fundamentalists; (4) the *creed* becomes a deposit of bizarre affirmations from which nothing follows; (5) the *code* is reduced to a series of apodictic irrelevancies; (6) the *cult*, or worship, is turned into magic; and (7) contemplative prayerfulness itself becomes a tool of passivity.

However, this corrupting process of routinization is forestalled and authenticity—genuine faithfulness—renewed when prayerfulness, especially mystical prayerfulness, is ascendant. Loyalty to the Holy One, expressing itself in action, is the result of what Karl Rahner called "the easiest and at once the most difficult existential act . . . the acceptance of this [God] ineffably loving and forgiving presence."[6] Such acceptance is "believing"; but believing, as Wilfred Cantwell Smith has pointed out, comes from the German verb "lieben," to love. The Latin, "credo," reveals the same; it is an amalgam of the noun for "heart" and the verb "to give": "to give one's heart." (Also, no matter how much contemporary Catholic Restorationists misuse the word, "orthodoxy" will never mean "straight truths," but always mean "right praise".)[7]

The love of which these authors speak and the praise of the Holy One which overflows in action emanate from the contemplative center.

To summarize: prayerfulness is the heart of faithfulness ("religiousness" if one wishes, but distinguished from "belonging to a religion"). However powerful the impulse to "give one's heart" which results from public ritual prayerfulness (and anyone moved in their depths by Eucharist ritual will not easily underestimate its power), nevertheless ritual prayer takes root in interior prayerfulness (meditativeness, contemplativeness of being). That all prayerfulness must originate in paying attention to the interior life is what Saint Augustine points to when he writes, "Descend into thyself; go into the secret chamber of thy mind. If thou be far from thyself, how can'st thou be near to God?"[8] This is the meaning of the ancient maxim of early Christianity, "Lex orandi, lex credenti," "the law of praying is the law of believing," not "pray real hard and you might get the grace to affirm the truth of a lot of doctrinal statements," but rather prayerfulness *is* faithfulness.

Placing prayerfulness at the center is the surest way to reform religion. Rahner is saying as much (and in the process supplying the operative meaning of "mystical" in this essay) when he writes, "The Christian of the future will be a mystic or he or she will not exist at all. If by mysticism we mean, not singular parapsychological phenomena, but a genuine experience of God emerging from the very heart of our existence."[9]

Only those in thrall to "religion" fear that influences from paths other than that of their own childhood religious socialization will lead to idolatry. Those following a genuine path of faithfulness welcome clues to experiencing God from religious traditions other than their own; indeed "their own" path is irrevocably changed. While they may remain identifiably members of a certain "religious body," their way of being in that body, or on that path, is never the same. This kind of openness to clues prompted Raymundo Panikkar to begin his classes in comparative mysticism by counseling the students "that if they were not open to the possibility of being converted during the semester they should immediately drop the course."[10] In a similar, not identical but similar, vein, Krister Stendahl speaks often of a "holy envy" of the beauty and inspiration of clues from paths of faithfulness other than one's own and identifies this feeling with genuine interreligious encounter.[11] One of the most striking instances of genuine interreligious appreciation, such as Panikkar and Stendahl point to, is Thomas Merton's discussion of Zen. In the essay "The Study of Zen," in *Zen and the Bird of Appetite*, Merton distinguishes between "Zen" and "Zen Buddhism."[12] In a discussion of Zen Buddhism, Zen can be studied as to *structure*; in doing so, one is studying Buddhism but not exhausting the meaning and experience of Zen itself. One might, Merton says, juxtapose this study with that of "Catholicism," in its structures and systems (not, to borrow from Rosemary Haughton, the "Catholic Thing" which is never reducible to "Catholicism").

"Studied as structures and systems and as religions . . . ," Merton says, "Zen and Catholicism don't mix any better than oil and water"; but Zen itself (like the "Catholic Thing") is not a structured reality available for study as an aspect of a religion. Merton quotes Dogen, the founder of Soto Zen, who calls anyone who reduces Zen to a school or a sect a "devil." Merton writes,

> Zen is consciousness unstructured by particular form or particular system, a trans-cultural, trans-religious, transformed consciousness. It is therefore in a sense "void." But it can shine through this or that system, religious or irreligious, just as light can

> shine through glass that is blue, or green or red or yellow. If Zen has any preference it is for glass that is plain, has no color, and is "just glass."

Merton finds evidence of yearning to serve the Holy One behind, below and always to some extent obscured by religion. He cites Barth's distinction between religion and faith, to which reference has already been made. He also finds the idea of mystic yearning transcending the structures of religion in Sufi experience of "Fana," "the extinction of the social and cultural self," and rising to the Holy One, and in Saint Paul's discussion of the "New Man" [Woman], in Moses' experience of the Holy One encountered as "I Am," in Rabbi Jesus' experience of kenosis (emptying) and in Meister Eckhart's teaching concerning "spiritual poverty."[12]

To Merton's examples of transcendent religious experience not reducible to, or fully known through, the study of the structures and systems of a religion, I add the experience of Hildegard of Bingin from the depths of which she can exclaim, "God hugs you. You are encircled by the arms of the mystery of God."[13]

It is the same power which is experienced, the Holy One, whether the language used is "Tao" (the Way), "Fana" (elevation), the Hebrew "devekut" (cleaving), Zen (meditation) or "New Being in Christ Jesus." Fear born of parochial values, no matter how understandable, should not be allowed to rob people in (or on) many paths of faithfulness of benefit from insights about practice of faithfulness from many other sources. Interest in the experiences of meditative or contemplative being is a powerful corrective, saving people from religion alone.

Theology

A theological apologia for embracing the practice of meditative prayerfulness, free of untoward fear of dissolution of communal identity, must include a critical examination of the role in the community of theological language itself. The need to do this is accentuated in the case of Christianity, given what have come to be considered the orthodox positions regarding revelation and mission.

One could wish that the enormously direct and clear discussion of the differences between "faith," "belief" and "theology" at the beginning of volume one of Richard P. McBrien's *Catholicism* would take root in people's minds and hearts with less difficulty. The treatment is very much in line with the classical, Western Christian definition of theology rendered in the twelfth century by Saint Anselm. Theology is "faith seeking understanding" ("fides quarens intellectum"). The Holy One is present to all creation, mediated through bread and wine, and lovemaking and toilet training and parental love and experiences of disappointment and "making the team" and having a pet die and so on. Faithfulness, in other words, no less than sinfulness, is not waiting for "understanding"; the complex, relational, graceful, sinful process of becoming faithful precedes conscious, deliberate, intellectual effort to express the experiences that give rise to faithfulness (and sinfulness). Faithfulness is occurring prior to, and then at some point alongside, theological expression.

It is as a result of the necessary beneficial but ambiguous, and sometimes destructive, process of giving expression to religious experiences in beliefs, employing theological language, that different ways of speaking of the Holy One and of faithfulness develop and fear of syncretism arises. An obvious kind of situation giving rise to such fear is when Christians, for example, are drawn to practice meditative prayerfulness by employing, again for example, the physical and mental disciplines of "zazen" (seated meditation in Zen Buddhism), or find themselves moved by the exquisite expressions of love of the Holy One in Sufi religious poetry. However, what lies below these fears is something more problematic than fear of syncretism. It is fear of placing prayerfulness of the meditative kind at the heart of faithfulness. It is this fear that gives rise to placing theological language, now transformed into "dogma," in the center. Theological language can, to some extent, be controlled; the contemplative heart cannot. What we get when dogmatic theological language occupies the center is the worst form of religion in the guise of faithfulness.

In his masterful anthropological study, *The Coming Convergence of World Religions*, Robley Whitson places convergence, itself a monumental development, in an even broader historical perspective. He attributes convergence to loss of confidence in a mechanistic explanation of reality, one in which reality is understood as made up, elementally, of separate substances. Whitson maintains that there is a dawning awareness of the processual nature of reality and the inevitability of unity. Of people raised in different religions, he asks, "If people begin to experience a positive confrontation of the heretofore separate religious traditions, what will keep them from acting or responding positively?"[14]

While Whitson's work is exceptionally sophisticated and in no way downplays the complexities of the coming convergence of world religions, he comes to the startling, but I think inevitable, conclusion that convergence itself, however much the sectarian spirit in religion may resist it, is prima facie evidence of meaningfulness in history:

> Put in terms of a religious commitment which presumes meaningfulness in history, the religious traditions have developed separately and now will continue their development together. They have a *further meaning together* [Whitson's emphasis] which we had never even suspected. It is not that we will discover that all along they were all the same. On the contrary, we must expect to find that their differences, so often accentuated oppositely to insure separation, are actually meaningful together, contribute to each other and constitute the new unity out of diversity.[15]

For all the clarity and inevitability of Whitson's conclusion, theological work, by and large, does not support the religious experience of those drawn to use all the clues they can to be faithful. Again, Whitson says,

> A test of theological perception into the issue of unity can be made of Christian theologians by examining the manner in which they approach the relationship between Christianity and other

> religious traditions. A certain benignity is usually present, but it is very difficult to find much more. With the rarest of exceptions theologians do not seem ill at ease with their lack of knowledge of non-Christian religious traditions.[16]

Another compelling view of the relationship between theological language and religious experiences which prompt Christians to embrace prayerful practice from paths of faithfulness other than their own is provided in Gustavo Gutierrez' work *On Job: God-Talk and the Suffering of the Innocent.* Gutierrez does not deal with world religions, but one of the central themes of his unique study of the Book of Job is the conflict between theological language and contemplative experience.

Gutierrez sees in the Book of Job support for the central methodological contribution of Latin American Liberation Theology, namely that theological discourse comes after Christian praxis: transforming, which is to say faithful, silence and action. He argues that a crucial question of the Book of Job is how to speak well of God, how, more pointedly, to speak of God in the face of the suffering of the innocent. To speak well of God, "benedicere," is to speak prophetic language and contemplative language; but first there is the question of speaking badly about God; and here the three friends of Job, Eliphaz, Bildad and Sofar, represent "theologians" who speak badly of God.

What Job requires is a language that gives understanding to his faithfulness. Job, in Gutierrez' treatment, comes to contemplate

God, to love the Holy One for nothing, which is to say gratuitously. Despite his suffering, Job goes beyond only hearing about God, what William James called "secondhandedness" and comes to see God with his eyes. This is the contemplative breakthrough: though still suffering (the happy ending of chapter 42, verses 10 to the end, is a later redaction of the text), Job is free of calculating theological expression intent on explaining God and suffering. Under the influence of such bad theology, God can only be either punishing the innocent or a failed cause.

Instead, contemplatively Job just lets go of trying to explain a God who lets it rain in the desert, who makes wild burros that no donkey master can tame, who creates ostriches. Job just loves God. He has rejected the orthodoxy of his three friends: that suffering is temporal retribution for evil action. He has adopted a prophetic language in coming to see that he is not the only one, or one of a rare breed, who suffers undeservedly; and he contemplates, he meditates prayerfully on, the Holy One: "now I see you with my eyes. Therefore I repent of dust and ashes [that is, I cease being sorrowful]." (Job 42:5-6)

A final observation about the tension between certain kinds of Christian theological discourse and openness to clues about spiritual potentialities from practice of many peoples on many paths of faithfulness comes from Elizabeth Johnson's wonderful new work of feminist fundamental theology, *She Who Is*.

There are few recent works that reveal with so much power and passion the problematic interplay of theological language and religious experience as Johnson's study contrasting classical language and contemporary feminist theological language about God. I will have occasion to refer to her work again, below, in the discussion of God and of Jesus Christ. Here I wish to note how Johnson contrasts metaphysical, hierarchical, triumphal and rationalistic theological language—significant features of the language of classical theism—with what she calls "wisdom discourse."

"Wisdom" (Sophia who, as Rosemary Haughton points out in *The Catholic Thing*, is at home to everyone and gives great parties).... Wisdom blows where She wills. The Holy One, understood as "Sophia Spirit," is alive and revelatory in the lives of many people, on many paths of faithfulness. If the language of classical theism is necessarily exclusive, wisdom discourse

> directs belief toward a global, ecumenical perspective respectful of other religious paths. The imagery of wisdom operates . . . to signify the play of God's goodness and just order throughout the world . . . Sophia . . . is people loving; her light shines everywhere, and those who she makes to be friends of God and prophets are found throughout the world.[17]

Christian Interpretation and Convergence

A theological defense of richly interreligious consciousness and practice requires examination of recurrent, even "orthodox," ways in which Christians speak about God, Christ, sacrament and the moral life. There are certain ways of understanding each that are not consistent with a richly, interreligiously nourished, path of meditative practice and contemplative being.

The motive here is not to produce a new version of the "God of the Gaps," this time in response to interreligious sensitivity instead of the so-called "advance" of science. In each case, a way of speaking about God, about Christ, about sacrament and about the moral life and its sources that is consistent with the unity of religious experience and similarity of practice also enriches Christian theological expression and, as often, retrieves a Christian tradition and theological expression which has fallen mute.

God

The Uncaused Cause, the ruling Caesar, the implacable Judge is not the God encountered in meditative prayerfulness; "he" is not the God of the contemplative being. (Not coincidentally, as Alfred North Whitehead said in *Process and Reality*, neither is this God the one revealed in the "gentle Galilean origins" of Christianity.)[18] The person striving for contemplative being does not encounter the God of classical theism in meditative prayerfulness, the God whom Walter Kasper characterizes as "a solitary narcissistic being who suffers from his own completeness."[19]

Peter Berger employs a distinction about images of God in the world's religions that is helpful at this point. He notes those images which bespeak "confrontation with the divine" and those which reveal the "interiority of the divine."[20] Clearly the latter is the imagery more consistent with meditative practice and contemplative being, but one should not assume that emphasis on the "interiority of the divine" inevitably produces morally vacuous religiousness. Such assumptions are part of the baggage which results in dismissing the mystical as necessary quietistic, monks and nuns as withdrawn, buddhas as detached and indifferent, Sufis as exhausted after their whirl. These are caricatures. The Sufi is still bound, as the literature of Sufism makes abundantly clear,[21] by all the Laws of the Qur'an, including that of charity. The Jewish mystic must still "do justice" as Micha counsels. A buddha is bound to practice *mahakaruna*, the greatest compassion. As to monks and nuns, we need only point to the example of Thomas Merton and Joan Chittister.

The God of the contemplative being, of one who strives gently in meditative practice, whether or not influenced by religious convergence, is captured in Elizabeth Johnson's interpretation of Hildegard's imagery:

> The Spirit, she writes, is the life of life in all creatures, the way in which everything is penetrated with connectedness and relatedness; a burning fire who sparks, ignites, inflames, kindles hearts; a guide in the fog; a balm for wounds; a shining serenity, an overflowing fountain that spreads to all sides. She is life. She purifies, absolves, strengthens, heals, gathers the perplexed, seeks the

> lost. She pours the juice of contrition into hardened hearts. She plays music in the soul, being herself the melody of praise and joy. She awakens might and hope, blowing everywhere the winds of renewal in creation.[22]

Christ

The Christ of meditative prayer and contemplative being is not primarily the first-century Palestinian exemplar of prophetic faith. Neither is he the exalter avatar, the divine Son, seated at the right hand of the Holy One. In saying so, I mean in no way to diminish the doctrinal or religious importance of these traditions of belief. Each of these emphases contains great value. I am myself, for example, most prizing of traditions of Christology which focus attention on the Jewishness of Jesus and, at the other end of the christological spectrum, the christic mysticism of Teilhard de Chardin.

However, it is important for those who wish to be comfortable with a *Christian* meditative prayerfulness nurtured by interreligious insight and practice to confront the relationship between apophatic prayerfulness (the silent, aniconic, meditative kind) and the *images* of Christ. Looking at Aldous Huxley's criticism of Christianity, his idea of the irreconcilable difference between Christian iconography (imaging of Christ) and contemplation can be helpful in clarifying matters.

Huxley maintained, in the words of William Johnson, that

> the genuine apophatic mysticism that came from India to Neoplatonism and was transmitted to the Christian tradition through . . . Dionysius, is quite incompatible with an orthodox and Biblical Christianity inextricably bound to the man called Jesus Christ. Catholicism, he feels (and especially that brand taught by the Jesuits), has a kind of prayer centered on meditation on the person of Christ, on His virtues, His qualities, His words—a meditative exercise which is incompatible with the superconceptual silence of mystical prayer.[23]

Johnson himself supplies a ready answer to this criticism. In *The Still Point*, especially in his discussion of Saint John of the Cross, Johnson makes clear that, as encountered in contemplation, "Christ is present *but not as an object of meditation* [Johnson's emphasis]: he is present within."[24] This is the state of contemplative absorption, in which Christ is not an object, which moves Saint Paul to say, "I live; no, not I, but Christ in me." Again, in Ephesians, Paul prays that "Christ may dwell by faith in your hearts." As Johnson notes, the Hebrew metaphor "heart" means "core of being" or "deepest self." So Johnson urges: "Let us at least reflect on the possibility that Christ can be known without ideas—that he can be known in the darkness, in the void, in the emptiness that transcends thought."[25]

The tension between contemplative cleaving to Christ and imaging Christ is not the only problem that needs to be addressed for Christians to feel comfortable maintaining loyalty to that which is specific to their religious path while at the same time cultivating openness to clues—both insight and practice—from other paths of faithfulness. The other great difficulty has to do with exclusivist claims about Jesus Christ and salvation. This problem needs to be framed in all its enormity. At one level a Christian sitting in meditative tranquillity, breathing in and breathing out, might simply appropriate a Zen gatha like the one that begins, "The bell of mindfulness in the voice of the Buddha calling us back to ourselves," substituting "Christ" for "Buddha." This is not a problem, provided the Christian not only "uses" but also grows in appreciation for what is used. The problem is that proselytizing Christianity is antithetical to contemplative Christianity. One cannot be simultaneously a triumphal Christian and a contemplative Christian. Trying to make the world over so that everyone is "in" one's own religion is psychologically polar to the practice of peaceful, composed, calm, compassionate, nonviolent, contemplative being.

The work of Paul Knitter is especially helpful in confronting the tension between exclusivist claims about Jesus Christ, and the Church, and salvation and the unity of religious experience.

In his book *No Other Name: A Critical Survey of Christian Attitudes Toward the World's Religions*, Knitter says, "The continuing evaluation of Christology will need to make use of one of the main forces that moved it forward in the New Testament period: dialogue with other cultures."[26] Toward this end, in confrontation (and convergence) with other paths of faithfulness,

Knitter urges Christians to entertain, not an "exclusivist model" of Christology nor a "normative model," but a "theocentric model." In this approach Christ is perceived "as a universally relevant manifestation (sacrament, incarnation) of divine revelation and salvation."[27] The approach is similar to that of Paul van Buren who says, "every proper christological statement, however 'high,' will make it clear that it gives the glory to God the Father [sic]."[28] Knitter's focus also calls to mind Whitson's idea that what is specific to different paths of faithfulness may enrich each.

Also, in a vein quite similar to Knitter's, Elizabeth Johnson, speaking of "Jesus-Sophia," says, "Jesus-Sophia personally incarnates her [Spirit-Sophia's] gracious care in one particular history, for the benefit of all, while she lays down a multiplicity of paths in diverse cultures by which all people may seek and seeking find her."[29]

"Holy Envy" and Utilizing Clues from Other Paths

I diverge from the agenda stated above (the discussion of God, Christ, sacrament and moral life) to insist again, as I did in the discussion of god images in classical theistic language, that the point made here has nothing to do with making Jesus Christ palatable—and pallid—to people on paths other than Christian, or to Christians who are in a process of changing paths, or to convinced Christians who can't "access" clues from other paths as readily as they might if only a doctrinal stumbling block could be removed! None of this has the remotest connection with what is "nice" or what is—ethically or intellectually—"easy." Repudiating triumphal Christianity is itself a moral obligation for Christians. Rather than being a terribly burdensome duty, it becomes a preference vigorously pursued by Christians who have been touched by clues to spiritual potentiality from paths of faithfulness embodied in other world religions. In other words, it isn't that one rejects xenophobia, in doctrinal guise, so that one can use techniques of prayer or meditation from other religions or in order to be civil. When one is moved by the compassion of Shakyamuni Buddha, by the yearning of the Sufi heart for love of the Holy One, by Jewish love of life, awe and gratitude, one pauses. More to the point, when one encounters the Holy One so richly revealed in the life of a Jew or a Buddhist, the idea that there is no salvation outside the Church is seen not only as obscene but as absurd.

Consider the clues for corporate Christian life that are contained in certain recurrent, thematic features of Buddhism and Judaism. In doing so, three cautions: This is not an exercise in Christian self-loathing, but strong points in each of these traditions are juxtaposed with weaknesses that appear in historical Christianity. Second, Buddhism and Judaism are obviously highly complex phenomena; the features noted here do not represent the whole story. Finally, the intent of this contrast is not to idealize but to appreciate certain features of the traditions under consideration and to exemplify Whitson's idea that the religious paths "have further meaning together," as they converge.

Classical Buddhist doctrine places great emphasis on a process of salvation which is occurring now. In contrast, no matter how much contemporary Christian theologians work to popularize the idea of immanent eschaton, the historical dimension of salvation (which is to say that in some sense salvation is occurring in time) the belief that we are being tested now for possible salvation later remains deeply rooted in the Christian imagination.

There are examples in the history of Christianity of doctrinal certitude being raised to such an exalted place that it is a virtual substitute for piety and morality. In contrast, classical Buddhism, as Buddha's story of the person shot with an arrow teaches (see page 44), resists the reduction of religious feeling to an urgent search for metaphysical certainty.

Christianity, in some expressions, has lapsed into a highly individualistic system. Classical Buddhism insists quite literally that all reality is linked. In the words of the contemporary Zen Master, Thich Nhat Hanh, the very nature of being itself is "interbeing."

In some manifestations Christianity succumbs to a destructive moral rigorism in which virtue and feverish effort are equated. In most expressions Buddhism insists that the good life is a matter of gentle effort in which harsh legalism plays no part.

Some expressions of traditional Christianity attach a penitential connotation to suffering, others a retributive explanation; still others, most scandalously, attribute suffering to divine testing. In Buddhism suffering is understood simply as the universal ground of experience, to be overcome through gentle, but persistent, effort like the ox mired in the mud but moving steadily forward.

Christianity has provided civilization with an elaborate moral argument for "just war"; Buddhism preaches nonviolence.

Finally, though authentic Christian belief can never say of the Christ what Zen Buddhists sometimes say of the Buddha, "If you see the Buddha, slay him," in order to point the practitioner in the direction of living their own "Buddha mind," there is something profound to be learned here as well. It is to reject the totemized, sentimentalized Christ whose worship sometimes distances Christians from Christ life itself. It is to such christic piety that Dorothee Solle alludes when she says, "the empty repetition of his name works like a drug: it changes nothing and nobody."[30]

Turning to Judaism, we may begin by noting that its radically monotheistic spirit more often than not forestalls an idolatrous focus on the synagogue or temple. This is a healthy, correcting clue for forms of Christianity in which church structure is perceived as sacred.

The Jewish reverence of peoplehood is an antidote to religiously inspired individualism. Judaism's focus on the goodness of all creation stands in contrast to various forms and expressions throughout its history of Christian-endorsed theological dualism: the tendency to divide reality into realms of light and darkness, good and evil and to associate mind with good and body with evil.

The refusal within Judaism to elevate doctrine to a sacred role keeps the focus on behavior without, however (as the anti-Jewish Christian theological stereotype would have it), conflating religion and ethics. (Regarding the stereotype, anyone who has ever read Rabbi Heschel's work on the centrality of wonder and gratitude in Jewish life, or who understands properly the sacramental reverencing which is the motive and effect of ritual halakha, will not make this mistake.)

Forms of Christianity which draw a sharp and (unlike Judaism) literal distinction between the sacred and secular, those suffering from what Gutierrez calls the "crisis of two planes," can benefit from the emphasis in Judaism on the profundity of the ordinary and the holiness above all of time, an insight at once contemplative and moral in its implications.

Sacrament

The idea that a sacramental focus conflicts with a contemplative one is in some ways similar to the equally erroneous proposition noted earlier, that Christians, precisely because Christ is for them an object of worship, can never clear their minds sufficiently to meditate.

In highly sacramental expressions of Christian faithfulness, such as Catholic Christianity, the danger of ritual action divorced from interior disposition is formally acknowledged. Up until recent times, for example, Catholics exposed to even a relatively elemental degree of instruction in doctrinal notions had heard of the distinction between the "ex opere operato" and "ex opere operantis" dimensions of the efficacy of sacramental action. "Ex opere operato 'From the work done' . . . [is] a phrase explaining how a sacrament achieves its effect: not only because of the faith of the recipient and/or the worthiness of the minister but because of the power of Christ who acts within and through it . . . . Ex opere operantis 'From the work of the worker'. . . [is] a phrase explaining how a sacramental . . . achieves its effect: not only by the prayer of the Church but also, and necessarily, by the faith and disposition of the recipient and the minister."[31]

Despite the distinction, there is little doubt that Christian sacramentalism, or Jewish observance of ritual halakah, or ritual in virtually any religious community, is perennially prone to what one author has called "ritual fussiness," or to magic and superstition. For myself, no instance better exemplifies this tendency than the current debate within United States Catholicism over pastoral educational practice around the sacrament of Confirmation. Commenting on the debate between those religious educators who favor restoration of the so-called "original sequence" and those who favor using the sacrament as a rite of passage for teenagers and young adults, the sacramental theologian Joseph Martos makes a comment of a more fundamental kind that pinpoints the relationship between change of heart and ritual activity, between contemplative disposition and sacramental celebration:

> If the sacrament is the celebration of the ritual, and not a metaphysical entity bestowed by the ritual, then there is no intrinsic necessity for the ritual to be performed unless it actually signifies something new and different in the life of the person who is the subject of the ritual. To believe that it does (even when it does not) is essentially a magic belief . . . The ritual of confirmation has no automatic effect such as fully initiating a person into the church, and it has no existential effect unless it actually signifies a real change in a person's life the way that being married or ordained does.[32]

Therefore, the first point to be made about sacramental life and nurturing meditatively prayerful people is simply that the two go hand in hand. Still, in contemporary sacramental catechesis, the idea of gratuitousness ("ex opere operato") of sacramental grace is split from interior disposition ("ex opere operantis"). By the time the distinction reached me in a Catholic high school in New York City in the late 1950s, the full wording of the medieval formula, substantially derived from Saint Augustine's thought, had been abbreviated. The classic phrase was not "ex opere operato" but "ex opere operato *non ponentibus obicem*," that is, "from the work done *for those not placing an obstacle*." What greater obstacle to the existential efficacy of sacramental engagement than to participate in (more likely watch) rituals that do not move the heart because the celebratory communal act does not take root in a richly mystical yearning, a yearning, as Rahner said, for the presence of the Holy One.

The second point pertains to the heart of Christian ritual observance, to the Eucharist, and the relationship between Eucharist celebration and contemplative disposition.

The Christian Eucharist is a symbolic affirming and fortifying of qualities of being which are cultivated in meditative prayerfulness and the compassionate action which flows from prayerfulness. Consider some themes that swirl about the Eucharist, both in terms of historical theology and of Christian practice. The chief ones are: (1) death, the ultimate act of letting go, and new life; (2) gratitude or thanksgiving, which is the root of the word from which "Eucharist" derives; (3) presence, as in "real presence" and (4) eating . . . an ordinary activity. A word on each:

Death, Letting Go, New Life

All the great religious traditions recommend dying. The Qur'an enjoys the faithful "Die before you die." In the tales of the great rabbis, Rabbi Nachem is remembered as enjoining his followers to "repent the day before you die" (die to an unrepentant self, the day before your physical death). His followers fell for it, of course, asking how they could know the day of their death, to which the Rabbi responded, "Then repent every day."

The great contemporary Zen Master Shunryu Suzuki wrote, "In order to exist in the realm of Buddha nature, it is necessary to die as a small being moment by moment"; and in the Gospel of John (12:26), Rabbi Jesus enjoins his followers not to try to save their lives but to lose them and in doing so save them.

The courage, the confidence, the peace that enabled Rabbi Jesus to celebrate seder with his followers under such perilous circumstances as those at the time of his final Passover are the qualities of the contemplative, one who practices letting go. The Christian at Eucharist can link ritual gesture and calm interior focus on letting go, on practicing dying.

Gratefulness, Thanksgiving

The Zen Master Thich Nhat Hanh says of the "mindful" person, which is to say the meditative person, that right in the middle of an ordinary day, with ordinary occupations, with its ordinary interplay of vexatious, peaceful and neutral happenings, she or he can be happy that they do not have a toothache.

One comes to the Christian Eucharist to nurture gratitude for participation in New Being in Christ Jesus. Lest the engagement become routine, the meditative Christian needs to cultivate the constant state of gratitude. In this regard Brother David Stendal-Rast's wonderful book is especially instructive. For Stendal-Rast, indeed for all those on paths of meditativeness or meditative prayerfulness, the prayer/the meditation is the constant state of consciousness of gratefulness. Thus, he names one of his books, *Gratefulness: The Heart of Prayer.*

Presence and Eating OR Presence and Ordinary Things

The central achievement for which all mystical traditions of practice arise is to instill the quality of presence. This is the meaning behind Rahner's moving statement, cited earlier in this chapter, that "the easiest and at once the most difficult existential act is the acceptance of this ineffable loving and forgiving presence." One of the interpretations given to the Holy One's self-description to Moses in Exodus 3:14 is "I Am Present," or "The Present One." The medieval mystics sought "the practice of the presence of God." Saint Ignatius of Loyola enjoins presence, writing in the Spiritual Exercises, "Do what you are doing." One of the great gathas (sayings) of the Buddha begins with this:

> Do not pursue the past, do not lose yourself in
> the future.

> The past no longer is, the future has not yet come.
> Looking deeply at life as it is in the very here and now,
> The practitioner dwells in stability and freedom.[33]

Rabbi Heschel speaks of an ineffable Presence which "inhabits the magnificent and the common, the grandiose and the tiny facts of reality alike . . . a piece of paper, *a morsel of bread* [my emphasis], a word, a sigh—they hide a never ending secret: a glimpse of God? Kinship with the Spirit of Being?"[34]

Consider now, a Zen Master commenting on the Christian Eucharist:

> In his last meal . . . Jesus held up a piece of bread and shared it with his students, saying "Friends, eat this bread which is my flesh. I offer it to you." When he poured the wine, he said "Here is my blood. I offer it to you. Drink it . . . " I think Lord Jesus was teaching his students the practice of mindfulness. In our life we eat and drink many times a day, but while doing so our mind is usually wandering elsewhere, and we really eat our worries, thoughts and anxieties. Eating in mindfulness is to be in touch with life. Jesus spoke the way he did so that his students would *really* [Nhat Hanh's emphasis] eat the bread. The Last Supper was a mindfulness meal. If the disciples could pierce through their distractions and eat one piece

> of bread in the present moment with their whole being, isn't that Buddhadharma [wise teaching]?[35]

Whatever else may be said of the Christian Eucharist, it is, when rooted in meditative consciousness, a rich ritual for schooling ourselves in utter presence to and participation in—really "being in"—the moment, the action and the materials. When one trains to pay profound and grateful attention to the bread and wine now, to experience the bread and wine now as media of divine presence, many materials, moments, persons and events become available as instruments of this divine presence. Thus it was for Rabbi Jesus in the food of his last seder: he is one with bread and wine, one with the Holy One.

The Moral Life

For those who know that the faithful life arises from the still point, there can be no effort to found moral life on fear, reward, law or intellect (in the narrow sense of a rationalistic approach to natural law). Under limited conditions each such impulse may produce good effects; in an even more limited way each may also actually inspire moral life, but not sufficiently. Where meditative prayerfulness is placed at the center of practice to promote faithfulness, moral decisions flow from the center of a peaceful, collected, composed, quiet, courageous, grateful, reverent, nonviolent spirit. Gabriel Moran points to this conviction when he writes this:

> Mystics are accused of fleeing the world and not facing reality. But . . . the truth is that the mystics not only "face reality" but embrace it, or rather are embraced by it. What is fled from is the trivializing attitude of grasping at goods that the human cannot carry beyond death, or demanding rights to the exclusion of other creatures. The moral and mystical journey is not to ideal and spiritual forms above the world but to the deepest, darkest center of the material cosmos where goodness bubbles up in gentle, just and caring attitudes.[36]

Kathleen Fischer makes clear what we know from the example of the great hunger and action for justice of renowned people of contemplation and compassion:

> Contemplation is the attitude of heart required by an interrelated world view. What the contemplative sees is that center of love in which all things find their uniqueness. Out of such an experience we learn to see the face of God in the face of every other human being and all of creation.[37]

I have tried in this chapter to speak of God, Christ, sacrament and the moral life, as well as the real expansion of meaning in religious convergence, in ways that promote a richly interreligious practice of meditative prayerfulness. In the next chapter, actual practice of meditation is discussed.

Chapter Two

Life Is Practice: Meditating

Introduction

From Marx's dictum that the purpose of philosophy is no longer to explain reality but to change it,[1] and Mao Tse Tung's advice that the only way to have true knowledge of the pear is to transform the pear, which is to say to eat the pear,[2] to John MacMurray's idea that life is action and the purpose of all action is friendship,[3] contemporary thought provides many examples of views of human life in which the emphasis is on practice.

Ancient thought provides equally persuasive examples of the idea that, for all the value of intention and reflectiveness and knowledge of ideas resulting from formal and informal education, behavior, moment by moment, is who a human being is. For example, the prophets of ancient Israel decried the notion that there could be any justice that is purely verbal even if the words form "prayers."[4] One of the earliest sermons of the Buddha deals with the foolishness of people who will not allow a physician to remove an arrow from their bodies until they have thought about the substance of the shaft, the kind of bird who contributed feathers to the arrow and the make-up of the arrowhead, thus putting off till it is perhaps too late the necessary practice: removing the arrow before it kills. Rabbi Jesus of Nazareth's disconcerting rejoinder to his disciples' request for the truth was to say, "I am the truth."[5] The medieval Catholic philosophy and theology of the virtues and of character are an edifice of thought supporting the emphasis on habitual practice[6] as is Ignatius of Loyola's dictum: *Age Quod Agis* ("Do what you are doing").[7] In our own time, Cardinal Newman has distinguished that which is "real" from that which is merely "notional."[8] Also, the Zen Master Shunryu Suzuki has written this:

> Doing something is expressing our own nature. We do not exist for the sake of something else. . . . All that we should do is just do something as it comes. *Do* something! Whatever it is, we should do it, even if it is not doing something. We should live in this moment. . . . Our teaching is just to live, always in reality, in its exact sense. To make our effort, moment after moment, is our way. In an exact sense the only thing we actually can study in our life is that on which we are working in each moment.[9]

Meditation is practice; a discrete moment or half hour of seated meditation is practice. So too is practicing, moment by moment, to become meditative. But what experiences give rise to the desire to be meditative and to practice meditation?

The experiences that give rise to this practice are the experience of "holding one's being" and the experience of "losing one's self." When people have the happy experience of being authentically self-possessed and reflect on the experience, they notice that this is not the habitual state of their living and practicing and the desire arises to be this way all the time; and, conversely, when people experience "losing one's self," there follows fear, anxiety, perhaps shame or guilt, and they want to practice not losing themselves.

Children, teenagers, young adults and adults lose themselves just before athletic events or before musical recitals, just as they are about to ask for a date or respond to an invitation to date. We lose ourselves while making presentations about new product lines, on check-out lines, when a child spills grape juice, when we see a companion brutalized by violence, when we lose an opportunity for advancement to another. People also lose themselves in traffic jams, while preparing meals, and in arguments with loved ones; we lose ourselves in a crowd and when we are alone.

Even people who live relatively privileged lives, who have enough to eat and a secure home, who have jobs and safe neighborhoods and who have some friends, lose themselves. (How much more those who live their lives at the *margins*, who have insufficient opportunity, peace, food, shelter, care; and how much more admirable when marginalized people hold their being.)

Even those mysterious people who seem blessed with "splendid temperaments" (in contrast to those of us who seem to fight irritability more as we age) lose themselves. Concretely, losing oneself is being, actually being moment by moment, under the sway of irritation, anxiety, fear, distraction, anger, insecurity and the aggression and violence—physical and verbal—which insecurity engenders.

To hold one's being is to be calm, composed, concentrated, stable, quiet, joyful, reverent, grateful, courageous, nonviolent, indeed compassionate and forgiving—in a word, peaceful. When people are irritable, they *are* irritation; when they are peaceful, they are peace.

It is difficult, and not always productive, to try to describe the experience of meditating and, more broadly, of being meditative; this difficulty and peril give rise to the Zen Buddhist aphorism, "Those who say don't know and those who know don't say." Still, in one account of the temptations of Siddhartha, on the brink of his enlightenment experience, on the brink of waking up, the Buddha-to-be dismisses forever the evil god, Mara, by overcoming reluctance to speak, specifically to teach through speech, and says, "Someone will understand."[10]

Without pretense, then, and with a clear realization that others who meditate regularly may employ different language, let me provide what might be called a phenomenology of the experience of meditating and, provided gentle practice is also dogged, sincere and continuous, of meditative being itself.

Meditating and Being Meditative

1) The first moment of meditation, or being—or recapturing being—meditative, is the experience of desire to *"hold one's being,"* not to *"lose yourself."* The response may be momentary, what is referred to later in this chapter as a "momentary meditation"; or the response may be the beginning of a fundamental reorientation of one's human practice, one's path of faithfulness. Likewise the occasion of noticing that one has lost oneself or that one is authentically self-possessed may be of small account, if any moment and action is so, or of great importance.

In this regard, consider two wise sayings, near prayers, or what is called in Sanskrit "gathas." The first is taken from Thomas Merton's book of free translation of Taoist wisdom, *The Way of Chuang Tsu*:

> Hold your being, secure and quiet.
> Keep your life collected in its own center
> Do not allow anything
> To disturb your thoughts.[11]

The second saying is from the Zen Master, Thich Nhat Hanh:

> Do not lose yourself
> In dispersion and in your surrounding
> Learn to practice breathing
> In order to regain composure of mind and body
> To regain mindfulness
> And to develop concentration
> And understanding.[12]

2) So, wishing not to lose oneself, or wanting to enhance the capacity to hold one's being, a person *stops* and seeks to be silent for a sustained period of time or momentarily.[13] In order to stop and to become silent, a person takes conscious possession of his or her *breathing*, first by counting with the quiet voice inside of the self, the count associated with inhalation and exhalation: "one on the inhale, one on the exhale," and so on. Perhaps the person breathes in and breathes out to the pattern of the lines of a short gatha: "Breathing in I calm my body [feelings, mind, activities of the mind]; breathing out I smile. Dwelling in the present moment, I know this is a wonderful moment."[14]

A person takes possession of her or his breath in this, or similar, manner because people know, or they make a rational act of faith, that "breathing is a means of awakening and maintaining full awareness, in order to look carefully, long and deeply, see the nature of all things and arrive at liberation."[15] In this the practitioners are at one with women giving birth, with Native Americans who refer to their whole life as their "breath path,"[16] and with all who pray, "Come Holy Spirit" (Holy Spiration, Holy Breath).

3) Quite naturally *silence grows, and with it composure.*

4) Then a person begins to *pay attention, look deeply and approach the state of presence*, just being there. This is the meditative state, what Zen Masters call "Mindfulness." It is akin to what Thomas Aquinas called "contemplation": *"simplex intuitus veritas,"* a "simple intuition of the truth."[17]

This is the heart of the time of practicing meditation; it is also, as noted above, the meditative state of being. It is not really possible, however, to give language to the practice of presence as it occurs in the infinite variety of encounters, exchanges, experiences, perceptions, states of consciousness and reflection and action, moment by moment during any minute, hour, day or week of a person's life except to say that while meditative people fall back and lose themselves, they are more commonly calm, composed, concentrated, stable, quiet, joyful, reverent, grateful, courageous, nonviolent, compassionate, forgiving—that is, peaceful.

It is possible and necessary, however, to speak a bit about this stage of actual meditation:

A person meditating has begun by taking possession of his or her breathing pattern, stopping and growing silent. On the path of paying attention, looking deeply and approaching presence, a number of acts of interior work may take place. One may simply dwell in silence; for the person who meditates to pray, this may be experienced as dwelling in the Holy One. As Meister Eckhart wrote, "In all creation there is nothing so like God as silence."[18] However, it is quite likely that people in meditation will become distracted by a sound, by their inner voice intruding a happy or sad, anxious or neutral—functional—thought. They may become distracted by a cough from someone meditating in the same space with them or by an ache in their left knee or by a pain in their back. The third part of this chapter deals with the various simple techniques for returning to steady concentration on one's breathing, on stopping, especially stopping the sound of the inner voice, and resuming silence so that one pays attention, looks deeply and approaches presence. Here it may be helpful to note a few techniques for resuming meditative calm and composure at a point of distraction:

a) A common method is to resume counting until the pattern of one's breath consumes one's consciousness dispelling distractions.

b) Another method is to pay attention to the rhythm of the music which is playing softly in the background, if music is playing.

c) A third method is to breathe in and out to the pattern of the stanzas of a prayer or other wise saying (gatha). Those noted above, by Chuang Tsu (via Thomas Merton) and by Nhat Hanh, are examples. Another one is taken from Buddha's sermon on "The Better Way to Live Alone":

> Do not pursue the past
> Do not lose yourself in the future
> The past no longer is
> The future has not yet come
> Looking deeply at Life as it is
> In the very here and now
> The practitioner dwells
> In stability and freedom.[19]

d) A person may engage in a brief period of what Catholic tradition of practice of the interiority of the spiritual life[20] calls "lectio divina," or "spiritual reading." (If this option is chosen, it should only be followed for a brief time.)

5) One is *present*, not dwelling, in one's consciousness and perception, either in the past or in the future, not concentrated on something that has been done or needs to be done, but simply

present. As noted in chapter one, "presence" is one adequate metaphor for fullness of being or dwelling in the Holy One. It is for this reason the saying arises from Tibetan Buddhism that "Nowness is Buddhahood."[21]

6) Being present, one necessarily *lets go*. This is not a jump with an explanatory connection missing. Consider this: to be present silently is to let go; there is no "something" in the past, no "something" in the future to which a person is presently attached by his or her consciousness when he or she dwells silently in the present.

One lets go, at this point in meditation practice, of consciousness of joyful and neutral entities, recollections or expectations of the past or the future: the recollection of a wonderful meal with a friend last night, the expectation of seeing a friend later today, the need to purchase calamari at the fish market later in the day. In letting go of past or anticipated future unhappy events and experiences rests both the chief *therapeutic* and *moral* function of meditation, for a person lets go—perhaps only temporarily, but the letting go can eventually become habitual—of such states of consciousness as bitter anger, hurt feelings, envy, above all envy! One also lets go of fear and anxiety and insecurity and therefore of aggressive and violent thoughts and feelings. And a person may refrain from *acting* on such feelings under the positive therapeutic and moral influence of letting go.

In Christianity the tradition reminds us to practice letting go of the seven deadly sins: pride, anger, lust, envy, avarice, gluttony, sloth. In Buddhism the equivalent are the knots, knots of forgetfulness of being (samjoyana in Sanskrit); these are: desire, hatred, pride, ignorance, stubborn view, doubt, attachment, jealousy and selfishness. At some point in meditative practice a person might breathe in and breathe out to the pattern of a gatha or saying of her or his own composition:

> Breathing in I am letting go of _________
> Breathing out I am letting go of _________
> This is how I practice.

In what is called the "Anapanasatti Sutra" (or scripture), the "Sutra of the Full Awareness of Breathing," a wise saying to which our sixth meditation exercise will be linked (and whose key gatha is excerpted in Appendix II), there is a wondrous and odd stanza which goes like this:

> Breathing in I am *observing* [my emphasis] letting go,
> Breathing out I am observing letting go.
> This is how I practice.[22]

I mentioned this to a colleague whose reaction was joy and wonderment and who said, "It's as if letting go is so precious and so delicate that one must observe it gently, not assault it." This allusive but powerful idea of "observing" is the center of what some consider the greatest of the primitive Sutras of the Buddha, the Sutra of the "Four Foundations of Mindfulness." In that document, the practitioner is enjoined to observe the body in the body, feelings in the feelings, objects of the mind in objects of the mind and mind in the mind. The idea is to overcome split

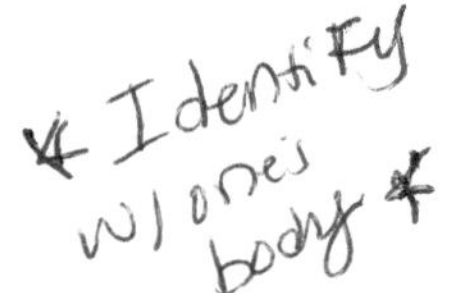

consciousness, to practice to identify with one's body, one's feelings, etc. (I am this feeling) and to enhance the capacity to really pay attention and look deeply.

A final comment on the sixth moment of this phenomenology of meditating. Letting go is an utterly central category of the language of paths of realizing spiritual potentiality. In Chinese religious philosophy it is expressed by the maxim "wei wu wei" ("non-doing doing"). Such maxims are easily used to caricature Eastern wisdom, whether with malice or good naturedly. The humorist Robert Benchley does so, good-naturedly I want to believe, in an essay, "Maxims from the Chinese." For example, one such maxim in Benchley's burlesque is "It is rather to be chosen than great riches, unless I have omitted something from the quote"; another: "Three cows are there, if only there were three cows . . . . Oh, Well, anyway—!"[23]

Despite the elliptical nature of the saying, making it liable for mockery, something exceptionally simple and important underlies the maxim "wei, wu, wei": action (which is life after all) done without mental and physical clutter is excellent; that is to say, the action is successfully, gracefully accomplished. People who seek to "kill two birds with one stone" have not practiced letting go; they have two things to do simultaneously; one must be let go of and done next (not however the killing of birds). Yogi Berra's famous retort to the question "What are you thinking of when you are up at bat trying to get a hit?"—"You can't think and hit at the same time"—is also subject to ridicule or good-natured putdown. But it is quite precisely so, cognitively and physically: one must let go of a certain debilitating self-consciousness, distraction or dual intent to act with excellence. This is non-doing-doing.

In Buddhism the letting go is the heart of the therapeutic and the moral effect: we let go of toxins, Christianity's seven deadly sins, Buddhism's knots of forgetfulness of being in order to be joyful and to be compassionate. It is precisely the same in Christianity in which Saint Paul depicts the divine-human interplay in Jesus of Nazareth precisely as letting go or emptying (kenosis).[24]

7) I have anticipated the seventh moment in meditative practice with the reference above to *emptying*, shunyata in Sanskrit. The linguistic distinctions are arbitrary, the two are one experience, in a life, in a moment of meditative practice. If a person lets go, he or she is empty of that of which he or she has let go! In a period given over to meditative practice, one does experience this emptying, not as words and sentences inside him or herself but simply as such. What is removed may be as simple as a low-level anxiety which one brought to meditation, as important as the reduction of physical pain; over a long period of time, one may let go of, empty oneself—one's practice—of some profound toxin, such as a consuming jealousy.

8) and 9) are elements in the phenomenology of practicing meditation which pertain more to the qualities of the self who rises from sitting in meditation, to what people take with them for the remainder of that hour or day or week, until again they lose themselves a bit—or a lot—and resume practicing holding their being. These qualities of practice of meditative being are *compassion* (which includes forgiveness) and *gratitude*.

To let go, briefly while practicing meditation, of anxiety over whether a store will be opened after work or, more seriously, having money to purchase a necessity at the store, does not extend the horizon of a person's compassion and gratitude all that much, although such relief certainly does not hurt. However, to dwell in calm, composure, concentration, stability and quiet—to be present and to let go, thus emptying oneself of fear, anxiety and insecurity—most certainly is the path of compassion. This is what the unthinking critics who label authentic Buddhism "quietistic" and authentic Christianity "opium" fail to recognize; in Meister Eckhart's words, "What a man receives in contemplation, he will give back in love."[25] To be meditative in a genuine sense is to be liberated from all that blocks compassion.

Regarding gratitude, this practice induces thanks from the bile ducts, thanks from the psyche, thanks from the body—the back, the neck, the colon—and thanks from the "heart." G. K. Chesterton said that humans need God in order to have someone to thank. Even those who meditate and who practice to *be* meditative and who do not have a name for that to which thanks are due are grateful for the way of being which is meditative and thankful for the half-hour of meditating.

Lesser and Greater Uses of Meditation

At the risk of falling into a kind of dualism which is the very opposite of the view of life and the practice of living which gives rise to meditative practice and practice to be meditative, it is nevertheless possible to distinguish lesser and greater uses to which meditative technique is put.

Among the lesser uses one might mention, there is the "Zen of Management," the introduction of management "retreats" to instruct employees about how to be more self-possessed while seeking to "close the deal." Management, of course, is wholly to the good. Who favors no management or mismanagement? Still there is, I think, a greater use to which meditation can be put.

Also among lesser uses, though here I begin to feel I may be bordering on denying the relationship of the realms of nature and the realms of grace, is pain management. Let us leave it that the use of meditative practice to reduce pain is a great good, not yet a greater good, and commend the reader to Jon Kabot Zinn's exceptionally powerful and moving study of same.[26] Let us also invoke Saint Irenaeus, whose famous statement, "Gloria Dei, vivens homo," "The glory of God is humans fully alive," legitimizes the use of meditative practice to enhance every feature of human practice which is good.

There is, however, the greater good in whose employ a person sets out to practice meditation and practice being meditative. Karl Rahner hits upon it in this, at first obscure but really very powerful, statement: "Anything is or has being in proportion to the degree to which it is subjectivity in possession of itself."[27] The subject to which Rahner has reference is the human person trying to return to, trying to conform to the Divine, the Holy Mystery which encircles us, holds us up, inspires—quite literally inspires—the life of calm, composure, concentration, stability, quiet, joy, reverence, courage, gratefulness, nonviolence, compassion, forgiveness—peace in us and in our acting. The greater good to which meditation is put is to cultivate being *this* subject, to live the life of the Holy One. Saint Augustine's injunction, noted earlier, fully reveals the greater good to which meditation is put: "Descend into thyself; go into the secret chamber of thy mind. If thou be far from thyself, how can'st thou be near to God."[28]

Practice

1) Guided Meditation/Simple Meditation

The goal of meditation is "just sitting," quietly, calmly, body and mind relaxed and at peace; being at peace we are, in the words of Saint Francis of Assisi, "instruments of peace." Guided meditation by definition is the intrusion of things—candles for example—and music and spoken words and the sound of the "bell of mindfulness." It is very important that individual practitioners, and groups of people who meditate together, *experiment* with greater and lesser "guidedness."

Speaking of the Soto school of Zen and its practice of seated meditation, zazen, Shunryu Suzuki says this:

> Our Soto way puts an emphasis on *shikan taza*, or, "just sitting." Actually we do not have any particular name for our practice; when we practice zazen, we just practice it, and whether we find joy in our practice or not, we just do it. Even though we are sleepy, and we are tired of practicing zazen, of

> repeating the same thing day after day; even so, we continue our practice. Whether or not someone encourages our practice, we just do it.[29]

The guided meditation exercises that follow in this book are in large measure inspired by the simple techniques of the school of Soto Zen and its approach to seated meditation. When practiced in a monastic environment, such practice may entail *koan* study, meditating on a rationally inexplicable puzzle, as well as *sanzen*, the periodic meetings with the master or roshi each day to be quizzed on the solution to the koan. However, to a far greater extent, the form of practice recommended here is what might be called "walking around" practice: simple sitting, breathing regularly, assuming a straight back posture and seeking, through meditation, to become peaceful. This is a mode of practice consistent with a busy, active life, with "walking around" in that sense. The emphasis is not on the one moment of breakthrough, the blinding awakening experience called satori, but on working gently but, as Buddha said, like an ox mired in mud, to escape anger, dispersion, unhappiness, violence. When practiced by a Christian who employs Christian prayer formulas, the method is very much akin to "centering prayer."[30]

Therefore, practitioners should experiment with techniques that truly deepen meditative stability and composure and promote the truly meditative life, a life of compassion and of calm, even while they remain open and receptive to the insight available in *well-guided meditation*, for not too fine a point should be put on the differences between "just sitting" and just sitting in the context of guided meditation. As Thich Nhat Hanh writes under the heading "Unfavorable Reactions to Guided Meditation":

> "Some people find the sound of the bell and the spoken voice during the sitting meditation session disturbing. Accustomed to silence while meditating, they feel that their peace and their joy is taken away from them in guided meditation. This is not difficult to understand. In silent meditation you are able to calm your body and your mind. You do not want anyone to disturb that state of lightness, peace and joy; but, if you are content only with this, you will not be able to go far in transforming the depths of your consciousness. There are people who meditate only to forget the complication and problems of life, like rabbits crouching under a hedge to escape a hunter, or like people taking shelter in the cellar to avoid bombs. The feeling of security and protection arises naturally when we sit in meditation, but we cannot continue in this state forever. We need the vigor and strength to come out of the meditation hall into life, because that is the only way we can hope to change our world. In the practice of guided meditation, we have the opportunity to look deeply into the mind, to sow wholesome seeds there, to strengthen and cultivate those seeds, so that they may become the means for transforming

> the suffering in us. Finally, we can also be guided in meditation to come face to face with that suffering in order to understand its root causes and be free of its bondage."[31]

2) Environment

The physical environment for meditation should be quiet and darkened. The floor should be carpeted and practitioners should sit in a circle or in rows facing each other. Shoes, knapsacks, keys, glasses—the "stuff" which is shed when one sits—should be tucked away out of sight. Practitioners should have enough room between them to feel comfortable rather than cramped. Candlelight, from candles placed at a few points in the room, might be used to give off a small bit of light, or a single candle in the middle of the room may suffice.

3) Sitting

Though lying-down meditation and walking meditation will be practiced in some of the meditation exercises to follow, the most common basic posture for meditation is to sit: to sit in a chair, to sit on a meditation pillow, or to sit with shins folded under a small bench with a small pillow placed on the surface of the bench and one's backside on the pillow.

The meditation pillow should be firm enough and high enough to allow practitioners to sit with a straight back with relative comfort, legs on the carpet, backside on the pillow. The bench should be high enough to allow a person to comfortably slide their shins under it but not so high that they can't rest their backside on the small pillow on the surface of the bench with ease. The chair should be such that one can sit up straight in it without difficulty.

Practitioners should hold their heads ever so slightly cocked forward, but with ears and shoulders in line, and should decide what to do with their hands. Options regarding placement of hands during seated meditation include (a) folded in one's lap, (b) palms up, one hand resting on the other, thumbs gently touching, (c) the prayer position, (d) one hand resting palm up, comfortably in the lap, and the other—palm up or down—resting on the knee of the same side of the body, (e) both hands resting comfortably—palms up or down on the knees. Eyelids should be closed ever so gently.

4) Sitting with a Smile

It is a common feature of advice that comes from Eastern sources to sit in meditation with a slight smile on one's face, not a broad grin but just the hint of a smile. The advice may subject those who meditate to ridicule as practitioners of "feel good" religiosity or New Age escapism. The criticism is without merit; the smile is practice of irony, the capacity to hold together the infinite longings and the finite possibilities of our lives without despairing.[32] Thich Nhat Hanh says that the practitioners smile because they are not "colonies of the non-self," that the smile is a badge of "self-authorization."[33] For Conrad Hyers it is, along with laughter, a sacrament of participation in the "humor of God"; he writes:

> One would never guess from reading endless volumes of religious compositions that humor has

> anything to do with God. The impression one gets is that God created *homo sapiens* but not the playful *homo ludens* or the good natured *homo risens*. The only humanity that comes through clearly in the vast literature of religious thought is *homo gravis*.[34]

So sit with a smile, at least occasionally.

5) Standing

I find it helpful sometimes to begin meditation practice by first standing behind my meditation pillow, hands folded in front of me in the prayer position and counting my breath before sitting on the meditation pillow. (See Meditation Exercise One for greater detail.)

6) Bowing

One Zen master writes of the bow:

> By bowing we are giving up ourselves. To give up ourselves means to give up our dualistic ideas . . . . Only when you are you yourself can you bow to everything in its true sense . . . you should be prepared to bow in your last moment; when you cannot do anything but bow, you should do it . . . . Bow with this spirit and all the precepts, all the teachings are yours, and you will possess everything with your big mind.[35]

The bow should be graceful, deep, slow, with hands folded in the prayer position and feet relatively close together; it should occur at a point at which breath counting has succeeded in quieting the inner voice. One approach to the bow is to bow three times, "speaking" with the inner voice three stanzas of a favored prayer, gatha, saying, special word or phrase which one has learned or made up oneself. In my own practice I sometimes bow in conjunction with this gatha of my own composition:

> I am bowing to *let go* of dualistic self . . . (pause)
> past and future self
> irritable and dispersed self.
> I am bowing to *let go* of knots of forgetfulness of being:
> desire . . . (pause after each knot), hatred, pride, ignorance,
> stubborn view, doubt, attachment, jealousy, selfishness.
> I am bowing in *gratitude.*

Some practitioners may wish to bow at the end of a period of seated meditation in addition to, or in place of, bowing at the beginning. When I bow at the end of meditation, I do so to the pattern and rhythm of these three invocations of the Holy One:

> "Come, Holy One, fill the hearts of the faithful . . . (pause)
> A clean heart create in me, Holy One, and a stable—a steadfast—spirit renew within me.
> Oh, Holy One, teach me to count my days rightly that I may have wisdom of heart.

[The first line is, of course, from the *Veni Creator Spiritus,* the second from Psalm 52, and the third line from Psalm 90.]

One may bow from a standing position or from one's seated position. Not all meditation sessions need begin or end with bowing.

7) <u>Breathing</u>

In addition to what is usually a preliminary—warm up—exercise of breath counting, it is also helpful to key the pattern of inhalation and exhalation to the rhythm of the music which is sometimes played during a meditation practice session. More commonly practitioners should breathe in and breathe out to the stanzas of a gatha, a prayer or the repetition of a special word or phrase, as noted above and demonstrated in the meditation exercises to follow. Here one allows the breathing to, in a sense, be the "inner voice," to do the "saying" with the silent inner voice. The breathing in and breathing out meld with the "saying" of the words.

8) <u>A Lighted Candle</u>

When engaged in meditation with others I usually place a candle in the middle of the circle of practitioners. Though the eyes are gently closed, some light is experienced through the lids and occasionally I open my eyes slightly and gaze at the candle flame. If one finds that the insinuation of light from the candle directly in front of one and about six feet away (when meditating alone or, as above, in the middle of the circle) is helpful in paying attention, one should sit with the body squared off directly in front of the candle so that there is no need to twist, however slightly, to occasionally look at the candle flame. Many people who meditate regularly have no need of the candle.

9) Music

It is best to meditate with music on occasion and without music during other times of seated meditation, as well as during the duration of a single period of meditation. The usefulness of music to meditative practice is very much a matter of personal taste. The same is true for the use of the *bell*, although even when music is not regularly employed during meditation, the periodic intonation of the deep, resonant, meditation gong or bell is hardly ever intrusive and can be the occasion for refocusing or deepening the focus of meditation practice. (See Meditation Exercise One for more on the use of music and for information on resources.)

10) Stuff on the Body

It is always advisable to remove shoes before meditating. One may also wish to take off a watch and ring(s) and empty one's pockets. Those who wear glasses should remove them as well.

11) Distractions

Carl Jung expresses a moving insight in *Religion and Personality* when he speaks of people who can love their enemies and feed the poor but who do not practice mercy toward themselves.[36] Practitioners must exercise patience with themselves, gentle, ironic understanding when they fall back into distraction, including even a long period, a minute—perhaps longer, in which they have completely left the meditative realm and are fighting some interior battle, giving so-and-so a piece of their mind or planning the menu for supper. Whether the distraction seems to arise from one's left knee, from a "Kah-boom" just outside the room or from the flooding of one's inner self with a previously banished anxiety or excitation, what is called the "mind wave" actually comes from the practitioner and should be gently invited to depart by the practitioner. It often helps to go back to breath counting or to breathing in and breathing out to the pattern of "saying" a favored prayer, gatha, special word or phrase.

Conclusion

I want to conclude this chapter with some words about momentary meditation, whether meditating is "for everyone," joy and meditative being, and what the person who conducts guided meditation might be called.

Momentary Meditation

The reason for actually sitting and meditating is to live a meditative life. The beginning of the day is, clearly, a privileged time to sit for some substantial period. In addition, however, practitioners should practice to *stop* throughout the day, especially on the brink of an activity, an encounter, a task which promises to contain some seeds of "losing oneself," and meditate momentarily. Techniques more fully explored in the meditation exercises of chapter three can be adapted to the shortened time frame of a momentary meditation. An example of a regular time for such "re-collecting" of oneself is just prior to answering the phone.

Whether Meditating Is "for Everyone"

Anyone with experience assisting others to practice meditation has come across people who say that meditation just isn't for them, that they have a temperament that makes sitting still impossible. I confess that this is a mystery for me. On the one hand such disclaimers are supported by the Hindu wisdom which designates four *different* paths (yogas) to nobility of being: the path of affection (Bhakti), the path of work (Karma), the path of intellectual inquiry (Jnana) and the path of sublime meditation (Raja). On the other hand it is very difficult to comprehend how members of the same species, subject to the same mind-body antagonisms, persons with whom one shares a broad, general cultural context in which busyness is a chronic and corrosive malady, can fail to experience meditation as crucial human practice.

What is certainly true is that trying to convince the skeptical that they need to learn to practice meditation so that they can grow, steadily, slowly, moment by moment, into meditative persons, is about as fruitful as asking the kind of wood, the kind of bird and the kind of ore that contributed to the arrow stuck in the body. Perhaps one simply has to say, with Romano Guardini, "Wisdom is the knowledge of the time that belongs to things."[37]

Joy and Meditating

A portion of a Sutra taken from an early sermon of the Buddha goes

Breathing in I feel happy
Breathing out I feel happy
This is how I practice.
Breathing in I feel joyful
Breathing out I feel joyful
This is how I practice.[38]

Also, in the Letter to the Philippians, Paul writes, "Rejoice in the Lord; again, I say it: rejoice."[39]

However, many people who meditate do not derive joy or happiness from their practice, or they do not experience sustained periods of such feeling. For some, meditation is the equivalent of hanging on by their fingertips to a modicum of composure, a modest measure of charity in their dealings with others, a shred of empathy with themselves, the most episodic feeling of God's presence. I am not talking about people on the brink of a clinical psychological disorder of significant magnitude. I am speaking of people who try, who even follow the maxim to try gently, to work well not hard at meditating, but who remain, through some mysterious mix of nature and nurture, moderately irascible, moderately anxious, moderately distracted and dispersed. For them, for all of us for whom this diagnosis is to some extent accurate, it must be said that there *can be no guilt about failing to succeed in meditation and meditative being.*

The possibility of feeling disappointed in one's "failures" in meditating is very real. To the extent that practitioners are inspired by and avail themselves of Buddhist resources and a Buddhist perspective, the radical voluntarism of Buddhist psychology comes into play. In its classical expression Buddhism is a religion without a deity. Though one can argue, as Elizabeth Johnson does in her criticism of classical theism noted in chapter one, that much God-talk is blasphemy, still spiritual paths which announce in effect, "You can do this . . . you possess Buddha mind," while they encourage effort to develop inner resources to live nobly, are also potential sources of anxiety and guilt.

The medieval Christian tradition of practice of the "spiritual life" led to the same excessive reliance on what Paul Tillich called "purposing," and with the same results.[40] Luther experienced precisely this anxiety and guilt, the inevitable result, orthodox Christian theology maintains, of the overestimation of human freedom.

On this matter, the Zen story of the four horses—the excellent horse, the good horse, the poor horse and the bad horse—should be kept in mind. The best horse does all it should simply at the will of the rider with no threat of the whip. The good horse does the same but just before the whip hits its skin. The poor horse performs but only goaded by the pain of the whip. The bad horse will only perform adequately under great pain. Comparing these horses to people sitting in meditation, a Zen Master says the best horse is really the bad horse:

> In your very imperfections you will find the basis for your firm, way-seeking mind. Those who can

> sit perfectly physically usually take more time to obtain the true way of Zen, the actual feeling of Zen, the marrow of Zen. But those who find great difficulties—will find more meaning in it. So I think that sometimes the best horse may be the worst horse, and the worst horse can be the best.[41]

A Teacher

In this book, hereafter, the person who conducts guided meditation is called a teacher.

The reluctance to use the word "teacher," which gives currency to the use of terms such as "facilitator," is the result of the denigration of teaching, as if teaching is telling people things; it arises from equating teacher with "schoolteacher," and assuming the worst kind of school teaching and, finally, it comes from the arrogant assumption that in any one space, at any one time, only one person is a teacher.

The most defining act deserving the designation "teaching" is "showing how." Whoever reads on, with the intent of using these meditation exercises, had better be meditating and desiring meditative being. The great Rabbi Heschel wrote, "A teacher is either a witness or a stranger."[42] No one can be a teacher of meditation and a stranger to the yearning for meditative being at the same time.

Chapter Three

"Just Sitting": Meditation Exercises

Meditation Exercise One

The Humanity of the Body

Meditation Exercise One

PRELIMINARY ASIDE: The introduction is directed to the reader; however, a teacher of meditation may wish to employ some of this explanation and exposition at the beginning of the first session. Hereafter, asides to the reader will appear in this typeface, though again there may be suggestions in this type that can with benefit also be shared during practice sessions. Script appearing in the regular typeface is intended to approximate what a teacher might say in guidance to participants in practice. Please note one very important point in guiding meditation: it is crucial to stay alert over the course of a series of meditation exercise sessions to how useful it is to begin sessions with substantial discussion or to begin, after only a few suggestions, with meditation practice itself. In my experience it is likely that early on in a sustained period of regular, meditative practice, participants will express the desire to begin sessions with 25 minutes or so of seated meditation prefaced by the shortest and simplest of composing and prayerful initial remarks.

Introduction

The subtitle of this meditation practice session is taken from the conversations between Bill Moyers and the late Joseph Campbell which have been collected in the book, *The Power of Myth*. On television Campbell points to his head and says that "this," the mind, by which he means western notions of controlling our lives through technical rationality, is "a secondary organ." He then goes on to say that unless one "listens to the humanity of the body," one is liable to have a breakdown.[1]

Beginning

We are going to begin the meditation exercise by listening to the "humanity of the body," that is by practicing relaxation. Relaxation is not the privileged domain of those with sufficient discretionary income to afford long periods of rest and recreation. In fact, very little contemporary recreation is relaxing.[2] Relaxation is a prerequisite for stable and caring human relations, for passing tests, for success in our occupations and for prayer. Meditation itself is a mode of relaxation; however, in this first session we are going to pay particular attention to bodily relaxation and to a visualization exercise that underlines the need to gently cultivate the capacity to relax our bodies and thereby relax our minds.

The relaxation exercise which follows is taken from the book, *Visualization for Change*, by Patrick Fanning.[3]

Place your blankets on the floor, allowing sufficient space so that each feels comfortable that you are not crammed too near any other participant; as you were informed, though the floor is carpeted, the blanket will afford extra comfort.

After dimming the light and lighting candles, including the candle in the middle of the circle of practitioners, and putting on the music for this part of session one, lead participants through the relaxation exercise excerpted in Appendix I. Continue to breathe gently, rhythmically. . . . Now recite the following gatha of Thich Nhat Hanh, pausing between each of the five stanzas for about a minute and a half:

Breathing in, I know I am breathing in
Breathing out, I know I am breathing
out...(pause)
Breathing in, I see myself as a flower
Breathing out, I feel fresh...(pause)
Breathing in, I see myself as a mountain
Breathing out, I feel solid...(pause)
Breathing in, I see myself as still water

Breathing out, I reflect things as they are...(pause)
Breathing in, I see myself as space
Breathing out, I feel free...[4](pause)

[And at 20–second intervals:]

Flower .... (pause) .... fresh
Mountain ...... (pause) .... solid
Still water ...... (pause) .... reflect things as they are
Space .... (pause) .... I feel free.

The music played during this initial relaxation and visualization exercise is an original composition by David Ison, part of a series of tapes called "The Musical Body Program."[5] Ison has composed a series of eight compositions, seven associated with the classical Hindu wisdom about the seven regions of energy and creativity within the body. The seven Chakras: (1) Base of the Spine, (2) Abdomen, (3) Solar Plexus, (4) Heart, (5) Throat and Neck, (6) Brow, and (7) Crown. The eighth piece, played during this exercise, is called "The Harmonizer," a synthesis of elements from each of the other compositions. The music of the eight compositions of "The Musical Body Program" is a remarkable resource for conscious breathing, composure of the body and the mind, and meditative practice. Other music, for example, Steven Halpern's *"Eastern Peace,"* can be substituted.

Let's take a few minutes to gently sit up, open our eyes, reacquaint ourselves with this physical environment, continue to relax and converse. We will reassemble for meditation in ten minutes.

Though there are many postures in which to meditate, and very little "orthodoxy" about meditation, except for certain indispensable elements having to do with conscious, steady, deep, gentle, rhythmic breathing and with a posture that conduces to a straight back, I've asked you to begin this session by assuming a seated meditation posture, utilizing a meditation pillow, bench or chair.

Stand behind your pillow, stand erectly, not artificially but with a certain ease and comfort, feet together, hands raised in the traditional western Christian prayer position, which is also the traditional placing of the hands for the greeting, "Namaste," in India; (the term translates, "I salute the divinity in you"). Remember the relaxation exercise and take note of whether your hands, palms and fingers, are relaxed or tense; if they are tense, invite them to relax.[6] Also, regarding your whole body, move around in place, shrug your shoulders if that helps to ensure that your standing posture is a comfortable one, that you feel balanced, that your feet, while close together, are not so close as to throw you off balance but not so far apart that your stance lacks grace.

Close your eyelids gently and begin to count your breaths: one on the inhale—with the silent voice of your inner self—one on the exhale—two on the inhale—two on the exhale, deeply, gently, rhythmically—up to the number seven. Repeat the counting exercise and remain standing over your meditation pillow until you have achieved a certain quieting of the inner voice, until you are, at least for the moment, quiet inside.

Bow slowly, gracefully, deeply, three times, taking as much time, within reason, as you wish between bows; see chapter two for more on the bow preceding sitting.

Sit down on your pillow, bench or chair and continue to breathe consciously, to grow silent, to pay attention, look deeply, be present, let go, be empty. Those sitting on a pillow may sit crossed-legged or, with a population of people with relatively young resilient bodies, in the semi-lotus or full lotus position—options that will have been discussed already. Note that the semi-lotus position requires only a modest amount of bodily flexibility and yet is a great improvement—as a steady, mountain-like posture—on simply sitting cross-legged. Teacher is quiet now and puts on background music, for example, the "heart" composition from David Ison's "The Musical Body Program."

Teacher allows perhaps three or four minutes to elapse and then in a gentle, slow voice, speaks the following gatha, also from Thich Nhat Hanh:

Breathing in, I calm my body
Breathing out, I smile...(pause)
Dwelling in the present moment
I know this is a wonderful moment...(pause)

Pause between one and two minutes between stanzas of this gatha, depending upon how you gauge the comfort of the participants with meditation at this point...how little or much coughing and shifting is occurring.

Breathing in, I calm my feeling
Breathing out, I smile...(pause)
Dwelling in the present moment
I know this is a wonderful moment...(pause)

One- to two-minute pause

Breathing in, I calm the activities—the stuff—of
my mind
Breathing out, I smile...(pause)
Dwelling in the present moment
I know this is a wonderful moment

One- to two-minute pause

Breathing in, I calm my mind
Breathing out, I smile...(pause)
Dwelling in the present moment
I know this is a wonderful moment."[7]

Conclusion of Meditative Practice Session

Kindly place your hands, once again in the "prayer" or "Namaste" position, and attend consciously to your breathing, "breathing in...I know I am breathing in...breathing out I know I am breathing out...." Breathe in and breathe out to this prayer....(pause):

> Come, Holy One, fill the *hearts* of the faithful...(pause)
> A clean *heart* create in me, oh Holy One, and a steadfast—a stable—spirit renew within me [Psalm 52]...(pause)
> Oh, Holy One, teach me to count my days rightly...that I may have wisdom of heart... [Psalm 90] (pause)

Pause a full minute and conclude meditation practice by saying:

> Hold Your Being...(pause)...secure and quiet...(pause)
> Keep your life collected...(pause)...in its own center...(pause)
> Do not allow anything...(pause)...to disturb your thoughts."[8]

Teacher may end the meditation practice session by offering the benediction, "Namaste" or "Peace be with you," and thanking the participants for meditating with one another and with a teacher. PLEASE NOTE: this is a long guided meditation session because of the extensive relaxation session at the beginning. Discretion is advised.

Concluding Discussion: After inviting participants to slowly, gently "come out" of their state of meditative concentration in the same manner as the invitation after the initial relaxation and visualization exercise above, get a conversation going along these lines:

1) free-flowing conversation about the experience of meditation;

2) expression of opinion about what elements of the "guidedness" of the meditation, bow, intonation of sayings, music, candle, etc., were helpful, which were distracting;

3) when, precisely, participants plan on "finding time" during the intervening period of time between now and the next session to meditate. This should include a discussion of the <u>regularity</u> they will aim for and, very importantly, regularly recurring occasions in their "average" week, or whatever period of time, when their composure, peacefulness and concentration would benefit from a "moment of meditation," that is, stopping and collecting oneself, closing one's eyes gently, counting breaths to the three count, perhaps "saying" a short gatha or prayer and then proceeding with the activity they are either in or about to commence. If this book has been placed in the participants' hands and if some or many of them belong to Christian communities in which Eucharist worship plays a prominent role, a teacher

might encourage them to review the exposition in chapter one regarding the Eucharist and to sit in meditative composure prior to next participating in this ritual.

Meditation Exercise Two

Hold Your Being, Do Not Lose Yourself

Meditation Exercise Two

Introduction

Before introducing this meditation exercise, a conversation should be encouraged about the practice of meditation in which the participants engaged during the period of time since the last session. The interval between guided meditation exercises should not, of course, be inordinately long.

Before readying the room for meditation, I think we should talk with one another for a few minutes about breathing. We can't talk about the power of taking conscious possession of our breathing too much; (well perhaps we can, but we can afford a little more conversation about it at this point).

It must be hard for the beginner in meditation or meditative prayer to accept the idea from Zen Buddhism that to take possession of one's breathing is to be in healthy, not isolated but healthy, possession of oneself—that to lose your breath, to forget you are breathing, to breathe in little, feverish gulps, is to lose yourself. In Christianity we might say not to live in the presence of God, the Holy One, is to lose one's true self, or to lose consciousness of Christ life, "New Being," in oneself is to lose oneself. However, in Zen Buddhism, calm, composed, concentrated, stable, silent, reverent, secure, non-violent, courageous, grateful, peaceful life is a matter of learning to habitually be in possession of one's breathing.

It must be difficult, as well, for socially responsible people who see suffering and seek to heal it to accept, with patience, that the gateway to compassion is possession of one's breathing. In his wonderful book on meditative being, *The Miracle of Mindfulness*, Thich Nhat Hanh says, quite simply, "Breathing is Mindfulness";[1] and Mindfulness, of course, for all the theological distinctions that can be made, is the word in Zen Buddhism that corresponds to "New Being" in Christ Jesus for the Christian.

No one can prove to anyone else through argumentation how healing the habit of conscious breathing is, how much peace it induces, how that peace becomes contagious in human relations and radiates out enabling the meditative person to be an actively compassionate person. As the stories of the Buddha discouraging metaphysical speculation and of Jesus pointing to the personification of truth in his person teach us, you simply must practice, gently but with perseverance, and you will know the power of conscious breathing.

This session, we will focus on breathing and *gathas, sayings or prayers*; that is, we will focus on practicing to become good at regulating the pattern of breathing and conforming it to the sound, spoken by a teacher who is guiding the meditation, of certain gathas, so that one breathes in to a line of the saying and out to the next and continues in this manner. I will use three sayings, one from Taoist literature, one from Zen, and one from Christian scripture. These will be repeated during the course of guided meditation.

In lieu of steady, quiet, meditative music in the background during our period of meditation together, there will be periodic sounding of the bell. **Remember: use a bell that gives off a deeply resonant, composing sound.**

There is a very beautiful gatha, recounted by Nhat Hanh, which goes like this:

> The Bell of Mindfulness is the voice of the
> Buddha
> Calling us back to ourselves.
> We should respect this sound
> Stop thinking and talking
> And return to ourselves with breathing
> And a smile.[2]
> [Repeat this simple gatha again.]

Associating the Bell with Lord Buddha may mean little or nothing to persons who are not Buddhists or have not studied the life of Siddhartha and marveled at his wisdom. If you like this gatha, if it helps you let go of toxins and embrace peace, hold your being and not lose yourself, you might want to make a substitution at the end of the first line, for example:

> The Bell of Mindfulness is the voice of the
> Christ...or
> The Bell of Mindfulness is the voice of the
> Holy One...or
> The Bell of Mindfulness is the voice of
> Spirit-Sophia (recalling the discussion by
> Elizabeth Johnson of a more adequate theistic
> language to which reference was made in
> chapter one).

Whatever you do with this gatha, or whether you leave it alone, or however much or little the sayings I will speak during meditation dispose you to a steady, composed, stable, peaceful meditative state, it is time to pay attention in our practice to words, phrases, short prayers that can really compose the spirit, dispose the inner self to be peaceful and to act peacefully, which is to say to act compassionately. The theme of the special word or special phrase is common to and time-honored in many paths of faithfulness; you may be familiar with the *mantra*, for example, in Hinduism. In classical Christian mysticism, this resource for meditative being is no less prized. In the anonymous, fourteenth century Christian mystical classic, *The Cloud of Unknowing*, the author enjoins the reader to choose a word that will spread a "cloud of forgetting" of distractions, anxieties and the like:

> But choose one that is meaningful to you. Then fix it in your mind so that it will stay there come what may. This word [or phrase, prayer or gatha] will be your defense in conflict and in peace. Use it to beat upon the cloud of darkness above you and to subdue all distractions, consigning them to the cloud of forgetting beneath you.[3]

Beginning

Please stand in front of your chair, or behind your blanket, bench or pillow, close your eyes gently, and begin to count your breath, one on the inhalation, one on the exhalation, etc. When you are sufficiently collected, begin your bowing or, if you do not bow or do not choose to bow at the beginning of this session, simply sit or lie down. I will "invite the bell to sound" as you collect yourselves.

Once all participants are seated, as a basic calming resource, use an abbreviated form of the gatha used at the beginning of the first meditation exercise:

Breathing in I calm my body,
Breathing out I calm my feelings.
Breathing in I calm the activities in my mind,

Breathing out I calm my mind.
Dwelling in the Present Moment,
I know this is a wonderful moment.

After about three minutes of silent meditation, follow this pattern:

Ring the Bell and say, Rejoice in the Lord/Again I say it: Rejoice, pause/ring bell
Let everyone see how unselfish you are/the Lord is near, pause/ring bell
Dismiss all anxiety/from your heart. pause/ring bell
Present your need/to the Lord. pause/ring bell
The peace of the Lord/surpasses all understanding. pause/ring bell
It stands guard over your hearts and minds/ in Christ Jesus. longer pause/ring bell

After three full minutes: ring the bell and say,
Hold your being/secure and quiet pause/ring bell
Keep your life collected in its own center pause/ring bell
Do not allow anything/to disturb your thoughts. longer pause/ring bell

After another three minutes or so, as judged best:
ring the bell and say: Do not lose yourself/in dispersion and in your surroundings.pause/ring bell

Learn to practice breathing/to regain composure
of mind and body, pause/ring bell
to regain/mindfulness, pause/ring bell

and to develop concentration/and understanding.
longer pause/ring bell

Conclusion of Meditation Period

A teacher may wish to conclude the period of meditation by saying something like, "Thank you for meditating with one another and with me" or "Namaste."

Concluding Discussion: The concluding discussion should most probably proceed as in Meditation Exercise One, unless matters specific to this group of practitioners need to be addressed.

Meditation Exercise Three

Flower, Mountain, Still Water, Space

Meditation Exercise Three

Introduction

Before introducing the meditation exercise, a conversation should be encouraged about practice of meditation in which participants engaged during the period of time since the last session. Special emphasis should be placed by a teacher, leading the conversation, on the degree to which participants experimented with various approaches since the last meeting: different postures, short and long breathing exercises, differing gathas, mantras or wise sayings, and prayers "said" with the inner voice to the pattern of breathing.

Before readying the room for meditation, I think we should talk with one another for a few minutes about the bow, as well as short and long gathas, and the length of our inhalation and exhalation.

When I first read about the place of the bow in Zen practice, it reminded me of two things: the S'hma, perhaps the most revered prayer in Judaism, and secondly, T. S. Eliot's poetic fragment, in the *Four Quartets,* on kneeling. The bow, the S'hma and Eliot's reference to kneeling all invite us to pay attention, to look deeply at the role of reverence in our lives.

The S'hma is a prayer which Jews are enjoined to say every day, and even at the time of their death: "Hear, Oh Israel, the Lord your God, the Lord is One." In the poem by Eliot which I just mentioned, the poet writes that we are not on earth to carry rumor, to give report, to satisfy curiosity; we are here to kneel!

Finally, the great Zen Master, Shunryu Suzuki, writes of the bow:

> By bowing we are giving up ourselves. To give up ourselves means to give up our dualistic ideas. So there is no difference between zazen [seated meditation] practice and bowing. Usually to bow means to pay our respects to something which is more worthy of respect than ourselves. But when you bow to Buddha [Christ] you should have no idea of Buddha [Christ], you just become one with Buddha [Christ], you are already Buddha [Christ] himself. When you become one with Buddha [Christ], one with everything that exists, you find the true meaning of being. When you forget all your dualist ideas, everything becomes your

> teacher, and everything can be the object of worship.[1]

There are theological nuances as well as broad differences here between the affirmation of the S'hma, Eliot's piety and the Zen bow. But at a deep level they point to the same thing: being part of one (James' notion that the mystical experience is one of feeling united) being one, rather than split and scattered, revering, giving thanks for, cultivating amazement at that of which one is a part...being one, collected self, united with all being and with the Holy One.

> A teacher might remind participants that in chapter two certain prayer gathas that might be said to the pattern of slow, graceful bowing were noted; however, it may be better to leave participants to bow without words in their heads.

I also want to take note, briefly, of two points of experimentation with the mental and physical discipline in which we are engaged. I hope that if, like me, you are finding it necessary to employ *gathas*, sayings, mantras, both words or short phrases, and prayers, that you are experimenting, making up simple, short gathas. This past week I found myself sitting and breathing to the pattern of "Breathing in I am composed. Breathing out I am composed. Breathing in I am comical. Breathing out I am comical. Breathing in I am compassionate. Breathing out I am compassionate." Also, still on the matter of breathing and keying the breathing pattern to sayings, I want to recommend that you sometimes shorten a gatha or prayer so that the second time you "say" it inside yourself you breathe to the pattern of a single word or shorter phrase. This session, you will hear an example of this, as you have already in the "Flower, mountain, still water" gatha of Nhat Hanh which is repeated now. See page 103 for a rationale for the exceptional efficacy which I impute to this gatha/prayer.

Beginning

Optional: You may want to prepare in advance and obtain the video *The Practice of Peace.* Invite the participants to view the first ten or twelve minutes of a remarkable Dharma (wise teaching) talk which Thay (teacher) Thich Nhat Hanh presented in Berkeley, California in 1991. *(The Practice of Peace,* Parallax Press, P. O. Box 7355, Berkeley, CA 94707, 120 minutes.)

At the beginning of this talk, Nhat Hanh leads an audience of several thousand persons in a brief guided meditation which is keyed, as I noted previously, to one of the most powerful, profound and simple of the gatha poems of his composition.

Show the first 10–12 minutes of the film. The gatha, of course, is as follows:

Breathing in
I know that I am breathing in.
Breathing out
I know that I am breathing out.

Breathing in I see myself as a flower
Breathing out I feel fresh.
Breathing in I see myself as a mountain
Breathing out I feel solid.
Breathing in I see myself as still water
Breathing out I reflect things as they are.
Breathing in I see myself as space
Breathing out I feel free.[2]

Let us stand behind our pillow, bench or blanket or in front of our chair, close our eyes and begin counting our breaths and composing ourselves.

After a minute and a half, say:

Breathing in I calm my body,
Breathing out I calm my feelings,
Breathing in I calm stuff in my mind,
Breathing out I calm my mind,
Dwelling in the present moment.
I know this is a wonderful moment.

When you are composed, please sit or lie down.

Allow three or so minutes of silence; play music such as the "heart" composition from David Ison's "The Musical Body," or "Eastern Peace" by Steven Halpern, or comparable music.

Intone the following:

Breathing in I see myself as a flower,
Breathing out I feel fresh.
Pause 15–20 seconds
Flower . . . (pause)
Fresh

Pause 15–20 seconds and repeat at same intervals the full stanzas of the gatha and the shortened version (mountain/solid, still water/reflect things as they are, space/free).

After three or four minutes turn off music and intone:

Breathing in I see myself as lilies of the field
Breathing out I am secure invite the bell to ring

Pause a half-minute.

Flower	pause
Fresh	bell
Mountain	pause
Solid	bell
Still water	pause
What is real	bell

Breathing in I see myself as empty.
Concentrating on nothing, I am free.[3] bell

Invite the bell to ring three times over the next minute.

Conclusion of Meditation Period

Allow three to five minutes quiet meditation and conclude as in earlier exercises.

Concluding Discussion: In addition to encouraging conversation about the experience of meditation this session, a teacher may wish to invite participants to think about and discuss the exceptional relationship of the gatha to which the session was linked and insight about noble life from a variety of other sources especially from Christianity. For example:

Flower/Fresh

A broader interpretation of the injunction of Rabbi Jesus to model ourselves, in confidence, composure and trust, after the lilies of the field includes the freshness of being childlike. Sources as different as Gustavo Gutierrez, in his discussion of "spiritual filiation" and childhood in *We Drink from Our Own Wells,* Bernard of Clairvaux, for whom "natural simplicity"[4] is a necessary condition of holiness, and Friedrich Nietzsche, in discussing the transformation of the noble human person into a child in *Thus Spoke Zarasthustra,*[5] may be introduced in a discussion, now or over the course of a program of meditation exercises, in relationship to Nhat Hanh's gatha stanza "flower/fresh." There is, as well, insight available in relating the gatha and its call to cultivate freshness of being to the existential notion of *ennui,* a deep sense of boredom, purposelessness, giving in to what Rahner calls "the stupidity of the everyday."[6]

Mountain/Solid

This stanza can be related to Teresa of Avila's well known spiritual counsel, "Let nothing disturb thee, let nothing upset thee; all things are passing save the Lord thy God."[7]

A teacher might also note this notion, from Tibetan Buddhism, recounted by Sogyal Rinpoche in *The Tibetan Book of Living and Dying:*

> It is said that your View and your posture should be like a mountain. Your View is the summation of your whole understanding and insight into the nature of mind, which you bring to your meditation. So your View translates into and inspires your posture, expressing the core of your being in the way you sit.
>
> Sit, then, as if you were a mountain, with the unshakable, steadfast majesty of a mountain. A mountain is completely natural and at ease with itself, however strong the winds that batter it, however thick the dark clouds that swirl around its peak. Sitting like a mountain, let your mind rise and fly and soar.[8]

Still Water/Reflect Things as They Are

The meaning of this stanza really needs no further elaboration, though it could be related to the experience of unbreakable confidence in God's love which Paul articulates in the Epistle to the Romans.

Space/Free

The reference to "space" in this stanza evokes the Christian and Buddhist ideal of *emptiness,* around which quality a later meditation exercise will be framed. The reference calls to mind the saying of a Zen Master that "concentration on nothing is freedom" and of Meister Eckhart, that the "heart" of the Christian should be so pure, so empty, that there is not even an idea of God in it.

Meditation Exercise Four

God Has Made Laughter for Me

Meditation Exercise Four

Introduction

Before introducing the meditation exercise, a conversation should be encouraged about practice of meditation in which participants engaged during the period of time since their last session. Special emphasis might be placed on discussing whether participants utilized the bow during meditation, whether they are continuing to experiment with slight, but important, variations in physical and mental disciplines or techniques as well as music, candles, etc., and on experimenting with counting their breaths. This latter aspect will be important in a later exercise of walking meditation. It entails experimenting with what the natural count of one's inhalation and exhalation is, whether, for example, a typical, deep, resonant and rhythmic breath, neither forced, cut short nor unduly extended, is a five or a four or even a six count on both the inhalation and the exhalation.

Before readying the room for meditation, I want to share a few remarks about the *comic* or *humorous* character of meditative being. What I mean, quite simply, is that for all the variations of temperament associated with "nature and nurture," heredity and environment, and however differently it may manifest itself in one person or another, striving gently to practice meditative being—to be meditative—the practitioner will be humorous, will have a comic perspective, will have ironic consciousness.

What I mean is that a meditative person has *perspective*: he or she experiences this, that and the other irritant from within the context of a consciousness and perception which possess the quality of *hierarchy*: that is, the quality of seeing that not everything is as important as everything else. A great many potential sources of being irritated, scattered, angry, fearful and insecure, and therefore aggressive and even violent, can be "allowed to pass," not in a spirit of despairing passivity but so that energy, gratitude, stillness, composure, courage, compassion can be maintained. We train gently but doggedly not to respond to some sources of irritation, anger and anxiety, as Karl Rahner said, not so that anger festers in our hearts, but "so that it dies there."[1]

Whether it's "pie in the face" comedy or drolly understated humor, the quality of humor which is prominent in the life, the perception and consciousness, of the meditative being is this quality of perspective: to see our own striving, desires and actions against the backdrop of our limitations, but without despairing.

While Western Christianity has little to say about the virtue of humor, and a good deal of condemnation of comedy, there are these wonderful exceptions that point to the tradition's wisdom about the relationship between humor and "well-being." For example, the Book of Genesis has Sarah saying of the birth of Isaac, "God has made laughter for me; everyone who hears will laugh over me." (Genesis 21:6); and Dante describes the assent from Hell to Heaven as one from "misery to felicity." On approaching the eighth level of Heaven, he writes, "I seemed to see the universe alight with a single smile." (*Paradiso* 27:4-5)

Anyone familiar with the life of Thomas Merton will know what the point is. At the end of his wonderful essay, "The General Dance," Merton writes, "Even now we are invited to forget ourselves entirely, cast our awful solemnity to the wind and join in the general dance."[2]

Beginning

Our guided meditation will be keyed to another gatha composed by Thich Nhat Hanh and to an exercise of breathing in and breathing out to a self-developed gatha dealing with letting go.

Advise the participants that when we reach this point, one attitude, feeling, one "bit of garbage" inside us, should be the focus of each stanza of the gatha; that is, they breathe in and breathe out, mentally noting the same encumbrance of which they need to let go.

Let us stand behind our pillow, bench or blanket or in front of our chair, close our eyes and begin counting our breaths and composing ourselves, (or simply assume our seated position without first bowing).

Do not begin the exercise with music; rather for the first minute or two, invite the bell of mindfulness to ring at fifteen-second intervals.

If you wish, bow to the rhythm of your breathing.

When you are sufficiently composed, please sit down or lie down, unless, of course, you are already seated.

Put appropriate music on. After two minutes say this:

Be a bud, pause
    sitting quietly in the hedge. pause
Be a smile, pause
    one part of wondrous existence. pause
Stand here, pause
    there is no need to depart. pause
This homeland, pause
    is as beautiful as the homeland of your childhood.
Do not harm it please. pause
And continue to sign.[3]

Allow a full five minutes of silence, then say this:

Please complete the following gatha with the voice of your mind to the pattern of your breathing:

Breathing in I let go of ___________________
pause
Breathing out I let go of ___________________
pause
This is how I practice.
pause - pause
Breathing in I let go of ___________________
repeat a second and third time at 30-45-second intervals.

After two or three minutes, repeat the gatha of Thich Nhat Hanh, slowly, as above, inviting the bell of mindfulness to ring after each of the stanzas.

Conclusion of Meditation Period

As in earlier exercises.

Concluding Discussion: In addition to encouraging conversation about the experience of meditation, a teacher might wish to invite participants to think about and discuss the elements in Nhat Hanh's gatha:

- The whimsy of the metaphor for us, a bud sitting quietly in the hedge, as well as a conceptual meaning for the metaphor: that buds grow, that hedges are an example of interbeing, a gathering of living, cooperating, interconnected entities. This might be compared to Jesus' speech about vine and branches and Paul's regarding "mystical body";
- the smile, with possible reference to the discussion of the smile in chapter two;
- standing here, that is, the preeminent meditative quality of presence; and the homeland of one's childhood, that is cultivating wonder and simplicity;
- doing no harm.

Meditation Exercise Five

Walking Meditation

Meditation Exercise Five

Introduction

> This session is designed as a "change of pace," not simply because walking meditation will be taught and practiced, but because two films will be shown: the latter, shorter film dealing with walking meditation and the former, longer film providing an opportunity for participants to reflect broadly and generally on the meditative and mystical dimension of life in a manner that has not as yet been provided or encouraged in this series of meditation exercises.

At the start of this session, we will not be readying the room for meditation practice, since the mode of meditation in which we will be engaged [or which will be explored through film] later in the session is walking meditation, and the walking itself will not take place in this space.

If the film is available, say: First, though, I would like to show an exceptional film on the mystical dimension of life. The film is entitled "A Still Small Voice."

"A Still Small Voice" is a 45-minute video film available through The Center for the Study of Faith Seeking Understanding, located in Bethesda, Maryland. It is narrated by Bill Kurtis. The film focuses on *mystical* striving of human beings. The "mystical" is understood as the dimension, constitutive of human being as such, of yearning to live in conformity to a power available to human consciousness which enables transformation, feelings of well-being and of compassion for others. The range of spiritual, cultural and historical themes dealt with in the film is rich and should provide a midpoint summary of the profound, recurrent human yearning which is the basis for this program of meditation exercises.

Nature mysticism, theistic mysticism and *monistic mysticism* are treated as is the relationship of the mystical yearning to traditional practices in Judaism, Buddhism, Christianity and Islam, including Sufism. A section of the film deals with contrasting religious and scientific views of human striving for a truth that leads to human transformation. Another section deals with the inversion of the human mystical desire and its expression in violent and addictive behaviors, personal as well as mass movements, when separated from traditional religious structuring. There is a fascinating sequence in the film highlighting the work of the German anthropologist, Marie Koenig, and suggesting that the breakthrough of mystical consciousness—consciousness of ourselves as related to a higher power—is the origin of humanness. The film also has the benefit of presenting on screen a remarkable range of philosophers, theologians and mystics, including for example, the United Statesian Buddhist, Roshi Joseph Goldstein, and the English Benedictine, Dom Sabastian Moore. I recommend that a teacher sponsor a sustained discussion of the themes of the film after it has been shown. However, it may really be more useful to show and discuss this film near the middle of a three- or four-day retreat, but dispense with it in the context of a weekly meditation program. In this case, the session can begin with a short period of seated meditation and then proceed as follows.

Walking Meditation

For the remainder of our time together, I would like to invite you to view a short film in which the Zen Master, Thich Nhat Hanh, instructs a group of people in walking meditation. While we are not in a position to engage in walking meditation during this session, I think many of you found the short guided meditation session three on film, led by Thay Nhat Hanh, quite meditative despite the video medium. I think that if you view this film with erect posture, body composed, attentive to your breathing pattern, it will be a meditative experience.

Please note: Depending on the time of year and time of day, the session in which walking meditation is introduced may be a good one to vary timing so that the weather and time of day are congenial for actually walking meditatively and then reassembling briefly to discuss the experience.

The film, *"Guide to Walking Meditation,"* available through Parallax Press, Berkeley, California, is quite straightforward. In addition to this value, it:

• gives clear instruction on a mode of walking meditation that is quite consistent with everyday life and whose components (the walking, the counting, the breathing and the smiling) are explained with simplicity and clarity;

• opens out to the insight that all activity (preparing a meal, washing the dishes, making love, being in conversation, driving a car, preparing tea) can be done with mindfulness; and

• brings home with profound clarity that one walks meditatively, sits meditatively, prepares tea meditatively for everyone, not simply for oneself.

A teacher might wish to introduce, as part of a closing discussion of walking meditation, Gustavo Gutierrez' wonderful, and droll, observation, that in the gospels Jesus and his friends are always walking and eating, walking and eating. Gutierrez will ask, during lectures, what meaning should be given to the prominence of walking and eating. His answer is that these are signs of life; one cannot walk and eat if one is dead.

Meditation Exercise Six

Breathe, You are Alive

Meditation Exercise Six

Breathe, You are Alive

PLEASE NOTE: The remaining five meditation exercises of chapter three will not appear in the preceding format. In the first five exercises, script alternated between advice to the reader, set off by a different typeface, and suggested text that a teacher assisting guided meditation might employ. The point has been made; and the creative readers, including those who may use this book with benefit to guide others in meditation, really don't require that this format continue.

Theme for Guided Meditation

The theme for this meditation exercise is breathing. The subtitle in quotes of the exercise is taken from the title of Thich Nhat Hanh's translation of and commentary on Lord Buddha's "Anapanasatti Sutra," the "Sutra of the Full Awareness of Breathing."

Breathing has been spoken of in chapter two; instruction about breathing exercises, and teaching about the importance of conscious, steady, rhythmic breathing, abound in this text to this point. A teacher may wish to recall some of this, even while she or he again insists—gently—that the importance of this aspect of meditation cannot be overstated.

What follows is divided into (1) additional techniques associated with bringing breathing into conscious, steady, rhythmic pattern, and (2) the substance of this exercise itself.

Additional Breathing Techniques

• Long Breaths and Short Breaths: Sometimes it is helpful to take a deep, long breath, both inhalation and exhalation, to the count of a single number: 1 on the long inhale; 1 on the long exhale. At other times it may steady the breathing pattern and compose the practitioner to count multiple numbers on both the inhalation and exhalation, finding the number, usually 4 or 5, at which a full, unstrained but nevertheless deep breath in and out is completed: "1, 2, 3, 4, (5) on the long inhale, the same on the exhale. In an earlier exercise, in which Nhat Hanh's short film demonstrating walking meditation may have been used, such multiple number counting was employed.

It should be noted that the correlation of counting and breathing is always a preliminary or warm-up technique designed to create the initial stopping, growing silent, growing steady. It may be employed in the midst of meditative sitting, but this is virtually always the result of the need to come back—gently—from distraction.

• Fitting the Breathing Pattern and the Gathas: It is obvious by this point that peaceful, mental "recitation" of gathas, short prayer formulas, meaningful words (mantras) to the rhythm of breathing is a highly prized method in the approach to meditation laid out here. This is attributable in part to the weaknesses of the author's own practice; but, as alluded to earlier, the prominence of gathas, etc., is intrinsic to guided meditation as such.

Many beginning practitioners experience difficulty getting beyond an awkward stage of consciousness of breathing to a point where breathing is gently controlled but not inefficiently self-conscious. Part of this difficulty of technique has to do with literally "fitting" the gatha and the breath. For example, a three-stanza gatha such as:

> Hold your being secure and quiet,
> Keep your life collected in its own center,
> Do not allow anything to disturb your thoughts.

may not "fit" the duration of a breathing pattern. The practitioner may hurry the inhalation and/or exhalation to get the whole stanza "in" on the wave of breathing in and breathing out. Few generalizations about the inner pattern of meditation can usefully be made; but what is important is to note this difficulty, elicit some discussion, suggest variations. In the example above, I think that the most useful pattern is for each line to extend over a sequence of inhaling and exhaling:

> (Inhale) Hold your being
> (Exhale) secure and quiet,
> (Inhale) Keep your life collected
> (Exhale) in its own center,
> (Inhale) Do not allow anything
> (Exhale) to disturb your thought.

The same point of technique is related in crucial ways to varying the form of gatha, prayer, etc.: that is, shortening them in one's mental recitation.

• <u>Varying the Form of Gathas, Prayers, etc.</u>: A prayer phrase or gatha can be so prized that the practitioner experiences a certain reluctance to adapt it. The gatha or prayer then takes on the character of a formulaic prayer; one would not ordinarily, for example, shorten, adapt or add to the "Hail Mary." It is important, however, to encourage adaptation of gathas, and as noted in the gatha, "Flower, Mountain, Still Water, Space," Zen Master Nhat Hanh seems to encourage alternating breathing in and out to the mental recitation of the full gathas with follow-up "speaking" of the shortened version. Thus:

Breathing in I see myself as Flower
Breathing out I feel fresh
Breathing in I see myself as a Mountain
Breathing out I feel solid
Breathing in I see myself as Still Water
Breathing out I reflect things as they are
Breathing in I see myself as Space
Breathing out I feel free

and then:

(Inhale) Flower
(Exhale) Fresh
(Inhale) Mountain
(Exhale) Solid
(Inhale) Still Water
(Exhale) Things as they are
(Inhale) Space
(Exhale) Free

• Breathing Pattern and Music: No feature of meditation is more subjective than the perceived usefulness of playing music while sitting and of conforming the pattern of breathing to that of the music. The practice has little support in orthodox approaches to modes of meditation and meditative prayer of the centering kind; but it is very beneficial for some people, taking some beyond counting and beyond mental recitation of gathas and prayer phrases.

The usefulness of a musical component, the degree to which it facilitates conscious, steady, composed breathing, is in large measure related to the music itself. I have already noted that to date I have found no musical backdrop and aid to sitting that exceeds David Ison's compositions in "The Musical Body." His work is utterly unobtrusive and is composed to the pattern of human breathing; at least, this is how I would express its nature as a layman.

It is important to encourage practitioners who only meditate with music playing to spend some significant time experimenting with sitting in silence.

The Meditation Exercise

Since I rely on the reader to frame the guided meditation session in a manner similar to that already noted in sessions one through five, what follows is simply the text for the "guided" part of the meditation.

If the "Sutra of the Full Awareness of Breathing" (Appendix II) is obtained, participants should be given prior to this session a copy of the key gatha within and encouraged to review it, perhaps making it the centerpiece of practice during the interval since the last session. At appropriate intervals during meditation this session, the sixteen stanzas of the gatha should be spoken by a teacher.

The gatha lends itself especially well to practicing shortening the stanzas, alternating the full text with one word or short phrase.

Meditation Exercise Seven

The Holy One

Meditation Exercise Seven

Introduction

This is a good point in the course of meditation practice sessions to place substantial emphasis again on experimentation, the micromanagement of small, seemingly insignificant features of the side of meditation and meditative prayerfulness which is strictly athletic, which entails physical/mental training and discipline. Thus, for example, a teacher might encourage participants who have been sitting on a meditation pillow to try lying down meditation, with a thin blanket under the small of their backs to cushion the lower back, and with legs, head and arms not crossed but lolling freely on the carpet. Those who have been sitting in the simple crossed-legged position might be encouraged to sit in the semi-lotus position, a position which for many represents a significant improvement in solidity of seated posture, without however requiring a big jump in physical prowess, tone of limbs or practice of exercise. (Those who do try the semi-lotus position should be encouraged to switch legs, that is, to shift from right foot and shin tucked up on and against left calf and shin to the opposite, without undue concern that their slight movement will distract others.)

If participants have not tried meditating with a meditation bench (calves tucked under the bench, small pillow on top of the bench, backside on the pillow, and a slightly more cushioning mat under the knees), they should be encouraged to do so. Participants may also be invited to wrap a light, cotton blanket or its equivalent around them while sitting in meditation. (If it was shown, note may be taken of the fact that many meditators pictured in the film, *A Still Small Voice*, in both the Benedictine Convent in Oklahoma as well as the Zendo in Massachusetts, sat wrapped in something similar. One might argue that covering oneself with a blanket while meditating is psychologically symptomatic: is this whole enterprise after all an exercise in withdrawal into a womb? However, rather than being a psychological symptom, the satisfaction and aid to practice that so many find in sitting wrapped in a blanket, or equivalent, may be a theological clue that we are meant to be embraced, hugged by God as Hildegard says.)

Some participants meditate to nurture a "natural religiousness," the cultivation of their capacity for peaceful, composed, non-violent, joyful, reverent, courageous, grateful, compassionate being without reference to a deity. Others do not sink quietly into the center to encounter a Holy Presence because they don't know whether there is a Holy Presence. Many practitioners, however, are engaged not only in meditation but in meditative prayerfulness. The emphasis in exercise seven is on prayer, on encountering the Holy One in silence. Participants should be alerted to this and to the fact that more than usual, but it is to be hoped without undue intrusiveness, "spiritual reading" ("lexio divina") will accompany meditation during this session.

While the usual preliminary techniques for entering composed meditative consciousness are being accomplished, dispensing with the preliminary bow, but perhaps inviting participants to greet one another with hands folded in the "Namaste" fashion once they have settled into a comfortable posture, a teacher may slowly, meditatively, at intervals, read the three "rules" of centering prayer as set out by Keating, Pennington and Clark in their book *Finding Grace at the Center*:

> Rule One: At the beginning of the prayer we take a minute or two to quiet down and then move in faith to God dwelling in our depths; and at the end of the prayer we take several minutes to come back, mentally praying the Our Father.
>
> Rule Two: After resting for a bit in the center in faith-full love, we take up a single, simple word that expresses this response and begin to let it repeat itself within....

> Rule Three: Whenever in the course of the prayer we become aware of anything else, we simply gently return to the prayer word.[1]

A very well chosen Gregorian chant might be played very softly as background music during this guided meditation period or part of it. As the period of meditation proceeds, quiet, slow reading of scriptures which speak of the love and indwelling of the Holy One should be read in a cadence linked to the pattern in inhaling and exhaling. Three, from Jewish, Sufi Muslim and Christian scripture, are proposed here. The reading from Wisdom is not, of course, in the Jewish canon.

> For [Sophia-Spirit] she is a breath of the power of God, and a pure emanation of the power of the Almighty; therefore nothing defiled gains entrance into her. For she is a reflection of eternal light, a spotless mirror of the working of God, and an image of God's goodness. Though she is but one, she can do all things; in every generation she passes into holy souls and makes them friends of God and prophets. (Wisdom 7:25-27, RSV)

After an interval of perhaps three or four minutes, this Sufi saying:

> The whole world is a marketplace of love,
> For naught that is, from Love remains remote.
> The eternal Wisdom made all things in Love:

On Love they all depend, to Love all turn.
The earth, the heavens, the sun, the moon, the stars
The center of their orbit find in Love.
By Love are all bewildered, stupefied,
Intoxicated by the wine of Love.
From each, a mystic silence Love demands.
What do all seek so earnestly? 'Tis Love.'
Love is the subject of their inmost thoughts.
In Love no longer 'Thou' and 'I' exist,
For self has passed away in the Beloved.
Now will I draw aside the veil from Love,
[Those] who would know the secret of both worlds
Will find the secret of them both in Love.[2]

Finally, after another significant interval, being careful again to read gently, slowly and, as far as possible, to the rhythm of a normal, deep inhalation and exhalation, read the "lilies of the field" part of Lord Jesus' Sermon on the Mount, (Matthew 6:25-34).

Conclude by gently inviting the bell to sound and say, in the manner of Hildegard, "Most verdant people, (Pause) God hugs you." (bell) "Come Holy One, (Pause) Fill the hearts of the faithful"; and sound the bell three times gently at 15-second intervals, ending the meditation practice session.

Meditation Exercise Eight

Like Silence

Meditation Exercise Eight

Like Silence

The subtitle to exercise eight is taken from the beautiful religious aphorism of Meister Eckhart, "In all creation there is nothing so like God as silence." It has already been noted in the structure of chapter two that though the precise phenomenology of the consciousness of a person engaging in meditative practice can neither be expressed with utter accuracy and that it is probably not desirable to do so, something approximating that process is this:

1. the desire to hold one's being, not lose oneself
2. leading practitioners to stop and breathe consciously

3. and grow silent
4. in order to pay attention and look deeply
5. so that they are present
6. and, being present, let go
7. and are empty
8. achieve a great level of non-violence or compassion
9. and gratefulness
10. and begin again.

The whole unified experience is complex to relate (with the exception of the anxiety or hope that begins the process [step one] and beginning yet again [step 10] but is reducible in mindfulness meditation, as distinct from what some call "concentration meditation," to gently but resolutely achieving inner silence.

Words to this effect, the citation from Meister Eckhart, excerpts from Karl Rahner's masterpiece on those features of spirituality (a path of faithfulness) dealing with interiority, *Encounters with Silence*, might be brought to an introductory discussion.

However, early on, a teacher should indicate that this session will be the most sparse, that little by way of "guidedness" will occur, that simply dwelling in silence will be the special focus. No music will be played.

Participants having begun seated meditation, one simple technique will be employed three times. A gatha of Nhat Hanh, noted in an earlier exercise, will be repeated three times to a specific invitation of the bell to ring. Where in the gatha the term "the Buddha" appears, a teacher will substitute "the Holy One." The technique is this:

- After three or four minutes of silent meditation, invite the bell to ring three times at fifteen-second intervals.
- Say, "The Bell of Mindfulness is the voice of the Holy One calling us back to Ourselves..."; pause for ten seconds and invite the bell to ring three times at ten-second intervals.
- "We should respect this sound/stop thinking and talking..."; pause for ten seconds and invite the bell to ring three times at ten–second intervals.
- "And return to Ourselves/with breathing and a smile..."; pause for ten seconds and invite the bell to ring at ten–second intervals three times.

(*Note*: Allow approximately fifteen seconds between intoning the words in each of the last three bulleted sections above.)

After ten minutes of complete silence, conclude meditation practice by saying, "In all creation, there is nothing so like God (pause) as silence," and then something like, "Thank you, sisters and brothers, for meditating with one another and with me," or with whatever gentle verbal formula a teacher has already established for concluding sessions.

Meditation Exercise Nine

To Be Empty Is to Be Alive

Meditation Exercise Nine

To be Empty Is to Be Alive

Two elements are key to this guided meditation session: one is new to the whole course of practice; the other represents an effort, not too insistent, to encourage practitioners to commit the sixteen stanzas of the "Sutra of Full Awareness of Breathing" to memory so that it is always available to them as a mechanism for emptying their inner selves of toxins.

The novel feature is to invite participants during this session to acknowledge, during their period of seated meditation, one or more moderately or seriously irritating or deeply disturbing events, persons or situations which prey on the mind and dispoil peacefulness, and to work, meditatively, through these exacerbants. This is a common feature of meditation in the east and the west.

Thich Nhat Hanh speaks of it in his popular and profound work, *The Miracle of Mindfulness*. The great Japanese Roshi, Shunryu Suzuki, had reference to this exercise, writing in *Zen Mind, Beginner's Mind*, that one who had never sat (the simple reference to zazen) while suffering had really never experienced zazen, seated meditation.

Participants should be encouraged explicitly not to take on too much mental "stuff" during this part of the practice session and with equal emphasis to work through preliminary methods, ensuring comfortable posture, adjusting as necessary, counting their breath, achieving some undistracted inner silence before actually <u>breathing in and breathing out to the mental holding of the irritant in consciousness</u>.

Participants should be encouraged to develop their own inner gatha formula, but in this part of the session what is being proposed is that (1) the irritant be identified, then (2) the practitioner breathe in and breathe out in something like the following fashion:

Breathing in I acknowledge ______________
(anger over such and such, or pain caused by such and such, or hurt because of such and such)
Breathing out I acknowledge ____________
(the same)
Breathing in I am emptying myself of ______
Breathing out I am emptying myself of _____
Breathing in I am grateful for _____________

> (the participant fills in mentally something, someone, some situation, some relationship for which she or he is grateful—not to deny or cut short genuine, painful feeling but to practice being a grateful being).

Note Well: Unlike many previous sessions, a teacher guiding this portion of this session should actually intone such facilitating instructions as:

> Breathing in I am acknowledging a pain or anger or hurt,
> Breathing out I am acknowledging a pain or anger or hurt,

and then be quiet for an interval, and then begin to encourage the shift by intoning such leading instructions as:

> Breathing in I am grateful for this person, this situation, this gift, this relationship, this achievement, this grace.

This pattern may be repeated two, but no more than three, times over fifteen minutes or so before shifting to the second portion of the guided meditation in which at one- or two-minute intervals, a teacher intones the sixteen stanzas of the "Sutra of the Full Awareness of Breathing," sounding the bell prior to each stanza.

The session may be concluded a minute or two after the last of the sixteen stanzas has been intoned and time allowed to lapse so practitioners can repeat the stanza mentally by praying this prayer of Meister Eckhart: "Blessed are the pure of heart who leave everything to God, now as they did before ever they existed," and the bell invited to ring three times at six- or seven-second intervals.

Meditation Exercise Ten

Be Compassionate as the Holy One Is Compassionate

Meditation Exercise Ten

Be Compassionate as the Holy One Is Compassionate

Invite participants to adopt their meditation positions with little preliminary conversation, play music gently, and allow silence without intervention of a teacher for seven or eight minutes.

Gently, slowly, to the rhythm of inhalation and exhalation, read the following:

(inhale) When your mind is liberated
(exhale) your heart floods with compassion
(pause)
(inhale) Compassion
(exhale) for yourself (pause)
(inhale) for having undergone
(exhale) countless sufferings (pause)

(inhale) because you were not yet able to relieve
yourself
(exhale) of false views, (pause)
(inhale) hatred, ignorance
(exhale) and anger. (pause)
(inhale) And compassion
(exhale) for others (pause)
(inhale) because they do not yet see
(exhale) are still imprisoned by false views
(pause)
(inhale) [by] hatred and ignorance
(exhale) and continue to create suffering for
themselves and others.
(inhale) Now you look at yourself and others
(exhale) with the eyes of compassion (pause)
(inhale) like a saint who hears the cry of every
creature in the universe
(exhale) and whose voice is the voice of every
person (pause)
(inhale) who has seen reality
(exhale) in perfect wholeness.[1]

Over the next five minutes, every minute invite the bell to ring once and say "meditate on compassion."

After five minutes, say "Be compassionate as the Holy One, God, is compassionate," and invite the bell to ring three times at ten– to fifteen–second intervals bringing the session to a conclusion.

If it seems appropriate, after some discussion of practice, the course of meditative practice and meditative prayerfulness might be concluded with a quote like this noted earlier in chapter two from Kathleen Fischer's *Reclaiming the Connection: A Spirituality of Connectedness*:

> Contemplation is the attitude of heart required by an interrelated world view. What the contemplative sees is that center of love in which all things find their uniqueness. Out of such an experience we learn to see the face of God in the face of every other human being and all of creation.[2]

Appendix I
Appendix II
Notes
Index

Appendix I

Lie down in a comfortable position with your arms and legs uncrossed. Close your eyes, gently breathe. Now clench your right fist, tighter and tighter; notice the tension as you do so. Keep it clenched and notice the tension in your fist, hand and forearm. Clench the muscles for about five seconds. Now relax. Feel the looseness in your right hand, and notice the contrast with the tension. Concentrate on the feeling of relaxation. Repeat this procedure with your right fist again, always noticing as you relax that this is the opposite of tension. Repeat the entire procedure with your left fist, then both fists at once.

Now bend your elbows and tense your biceps. Tense them as hard as you can and observe the tension. Relax. Straighten out your arms. Let the relaxation develop and feel that difference. Do this again, and all the following.

Now wrinkle your forehead as tight as you can. Now relax and smooth it out. Let yourself imagine your entire forehead and scalp becoming smooth and at rest. Now frown and notice the strain spreading throughout your forehead. Let go again. Allow your brow to become smooth again.

Squint your eyes shut tightly. Look for the tension. Relax your eyes until they're just lightly closed. Now clench your jaw. Bite hard and notice the tension throughout your jaw. Now relax your jaw. Now press your tongue against the roof of your mouth. Feel the ache in the back of your mouth and down into your throat. Relax. Press your lips forward now, purse them into an "O." Relax your lips. Notice now that your forehead, scalp, eyes, jaw, tongue and lips are all relaxed.

Press your head back as far as it can comfortably go and observe the tension in your neck. Now shrug your shoulders. Keep the tension as you hunch your head down between your shoulders. Relax your shoulders. Drop them back and feel the relaxation spreading through your neck, throat, and shoulders—pure relaxation, deeper and deeper.

Give your entire body a chance to relax. Feel the comfort and the heaviness. Now breathe in and fill your lungs completely. Hold your breath. Notice the tension. Now exhale, letting your chest become loose. Continue relaxing, letting your breath come freely and gently. Next, tighten your stomach and hold it tight. Note the tension, then relax. Now place your hand on your stomach, pushing your hand up. Hold, and relax. Feel the contrast of relaxation as the air rushes out.

(Adapted from the *Relaxation & Stress Reduction Workbook,* New Harbinger Publications, Inc.)

Appendix II

1. Breathing in a long breath, he knows, "I am breathing in a long breath." Breathing out a long breath, he knows, "I am breathing out a long breath."
2. Breathing in a short breath, he knows, "I am breathing in a short breath." Breathing out a short breath, he knows, "I am breathing out a short breath."
3. "I am breathing in and am aware of my whole body. I am breathing out and am aware of my whole body." This is how he practices.
4. "I am breathing in and making my whole body calm and at peace. I am breathing out and making my whole body calm and at peace." This is how he practices.
5. "I am breathing in and feeling joyful. I am breathing out and feeling joyful." This is how he practices.

6. "I am breathing in and feeling happy. I am breathing out and feeling happy." He practices like this.
7. "I am breathing in and am aware of the activities of the mind in me. I am breathing out and am aware of the activities of the mind in me." He practices like this.
8. "I am breathing in a making the activities of the mind in me calm and at peace. I am breathing out and making the activities of the mind in me calm and at peace." He practices like this.
9. "I am breathing in and am aware of my mind. I am breathing out and am aware of my mind." He practices like this.
10. "I am breathing in and making my mind happy and at peace. I am breathing out and making my mind happy and at peace." He practices like this.
11. "I am breathing in and concentrating my mind. I am breathing out and concentrating my mind." He practices like this.
12. "I am breathing in and liberating my mind. I am breathing out and liberating my mind." He practices like this.
13. "I am breathing in and observing the impermanent nature of all dharmas. I am breathing out and observing the impermanent nature of all dharmas." He practices like this.
14. "I am breathing in and observing the fading of all dharmas. I am breathing out and observing the fading of all dharmas." He practices like this.
15. "I am breathing in and observing liberation. I am breathing out and observing liberation." He practices like this.
16. "I am breathing in and observing letting go. I am breathing out and observing letting go." He practices like this.

(From Thich Nhat Hanh, *Breathe! You Are Alive,* Parallax Press.)

NOTES

Introduction

1. James Q.Wilson. *The Moral Sense,* 1993.
2. Quoted in *The Alternative* [Newsletter] Vol. XX, No. 4, May 1994, p. 7.
3. Film Interview on CBS, with Carl Stern, October 1972.
4. Gabriel Moran. *The Present Revelation,* 1981.

Chapter One

1. *Ad Gentes,* No. 18.
2. Shaykh Fadhlalla Haeri. *The Elements of Sufism,* 1990, Introduction, [unpaginated].
3. Thomas Keating. *The Heart of the World,* 1981. p. 1.
4. James Douglas. *Resistance and Contemplation,* 1972, p. 53.
5. In Samuel Dresner (ed.). *I Asked for Wonder,* 1991, p. 40f.

6. Karl Rahner. *The Practice of Faith,* 1986, p. 39.
7. Wilfred Cantwell Smith. *Faith and Belief,* 1979, p. 133.
8. Quoted in Reinhold Niebuhr. *The Nature and Destiny of Man,* Vol. 1, 1964, p. 51.
9. Rahner. *op. cit.,* p. 22.
10. Cited by Harvey Cox in Peter Berger (ed.). *The Other Side of God,* 1981, p. 297.
11. For example in his lecture, "Can the Victim Ever Trust the Victor?"—the Third Annual Rabbi Samuel J. Fox Lecture on Jewish-Christian Relations, Merrimack College, North Andover, MA, April 20, 1994.
12. All quotes from Thomas Merton, "The Study of Zen," in *Zen and the Bird of Appetite,* 1968, pp. 1-14.
13. Quoted in Gabriele Uhlein. *Meditations with Hildegaard of Bingen,* 1987, p. 90.
14. Robley Edward Whitson. *The Coming Convergence of World Religions,* 1971, p. 50.
15. *Ibid.,* p. 52.
16. *Ibid.,* p. 11f.
17. Elizabeth Johnson. *She Who Is,* 1993, p.166.
18. As a characterization of Rabbi Jesus of Nazareth, his life and his teachings, "gentle" is, of course, not sufficient.
19. Quoted in Johnson. *op. cit.,* p. 166.
20. Peter Berger. *The Heretical Imperative,* 1979, p. 168.
21. Haeri. *op. cit.*
22. Johnson. *op. cit.,* p. 128.
23. William Johnson. *The Still Point,* 1970, p. 152.
24. *Ibid.,* p. 172.
25. William Johnson. *Christian Zen,* 1971, p. 50.

26. Paul F. Knitter. *No Other Name (A Critical Survey of Christian Attitudes toward the World Religions),* 1988, p. 181.
27. *Ibid.,* p. 172.
28. Paul van Buren. *A Theology of Jewish-Christian Relations: Christ in Context,* Vol. III,1988. p. 166.
29. Johnson (E.). *op. cit.,* p. 166.
30. Dorothee Solle. *The Window of Vulnerability (A Political Spirituality),* 1990, p. 140.
31. Richard P. McBrien. *Catholicism,* Vol. 1, 1980, Glossary, xli.
32. Joseph Martos. "Should the Original Sequence be Restored for Confirmation?" *Professional Approaches for Christian Educators (PACE),* Vol. 21, 1991-92 (March 1992), p. 196.
33. Quoted in Thich Nhat Hanh. *Our Appointment with Life (The Buddha's Teaching on Living in the Present),* 1990, p. 18.
34. Dresner. *op. cit.,* p. 28.
35. Thich Nhat Hanh. *The Diamond That Cuts through Illusion,* 1992, p. 63f.
36. Gabriel Moran. *No Ladder to the Sky,* 1986, p. 63f.
37. Kathleen Fischer. *Reclaiming the Connections: A Contemporary Spirituality,* 1990, p.18.

Chapter Two

1. Karl Marx. "Ninth Thesis against Feuerbach," *Collected Works,*1958, p. 507.
2. Mao Tse Tung, "On Practice," *Collected Works,* 1978, p. 146.
3. John Macmurray. *Reason and Emotion,* 1932.
4. For example, Isaiah 1:11-20.
5. The Gospel of John.
6. See, for example, Alasdair MacIntyre. *After Virtue,* 1981.

7. Ignatius of Loyola. *The Spiritual Exercises,* in Robert W. Gleason SJ, *Introduction to the Spiritual Exercises,* 1964, p. 21.

8. John Henry Newman. *The Grammar of Assent,* 1976, p. 158.

9. Shunryu Suzuki. *Zen Mind, Beginners Mind,* 1970, p. 30.

10. Huston Smith. *The Religions of Man,* 1954, p. 136.

11. Thomas Merton. *The Way of Chuang Tsu,* 1965, p. 128.

12. Thich Nhat Hanh. *The Miracle of Mindfulness,* 1988, p. 43.

13. At Parallax Press in Berkeley, CA, the publishing house that distributes Nhat Hanh's works, members of the Order of Interbeing who staff the press regularly practice "momentary meditation" as they pick up the phones in the offices.

14. Thich Nhat Hanh. *Transformation and Healing,* 1990, p. 46ff.

15. *Ibid.,* p. 52.

16. The Zuni Tribe of the present-day Southwest United States so refer to their lives.

17. Cited in William John, S.J. *The Still Point,* 1970, p. 133.

18. Quoted in Matthew Fox, *Original Blessing,* 1983, p. 133.

19. Quoted in Thich Nhat Hanh. *Our Appointment with Life,* 1990, p. 8.

20. The awkward term, "interiority of the spiritual life," is employed to avoid the conflated use of the term, "spiritual life," as if it were, in sum, the practice of interiority.

21. Sogyal Rinpoche. *The Tibetan Book of Living and Dying,* 1992, p. 67.

22. Thich Nhat Hanh. *Breathe, You are Alive!,* 1990, p. 8.

23. Quoted in Russell Baker. *Russell Baker's Book of American Humor,* 1993, p. 126.

24. Philippians 2:5.

25. Quoted in Fox. *op. cit.,* p. 237.

26. Jon Cabot Zinn. See, for example, *The Stress Reduction and Relaxation Program Workbook,* available through the University of Massachusetts Medical Center, Worcester, MA.
27. Quoted in Richard P. McBrien. *Catholicism,* Vol. 1, 1980, p. 148.
28. Quoted in Reinhold Niebuhr. *The Nature and Destiny of Man,* Vol. 1, 1964, p. 157.
29. S. Suzuki. *op. cit.*, p. 72.
30. See, for example, Thomas Keating, Basil Pennington and Thomas Clark. *Finding Grace at the Center,* 1978.
31. Thich Nhat Hanh. *The Blooming of a Lotus,* 1993, p. 8f.
32. See Gabriel Moran. *Religious Education Development,* 1983, p. 180.
33. See, for example, the videocassette, "Walking Meditation," produced and distributed by Parallax Press, Berkeley, CA.
34. Conrad Hyers. *And God Created Laughter,* 1987, p. 13f.
35. S. Suzuki. *op. cit.*, p. 43f.
36. Carl Jung. *Religion and Personality,* 1972, p. 32.
37. Romano Guardini. *The Last Things,* 1954, p. 104.
38. Nhat Hanh. *Breathe, op. cit.*, p. 8.
39. Philippians 2:4.
40. Paul Tillich. *History of Christian Thought,* 1968, p. 201.
41. S. Suzuki. *op. cit.*, p. 108.
42. In Samuel Dresner (ed.). *I Asked for Wonder,* 1991, p. 62.

Chapter Three

Exercise One

1. Joseph Campbell and Bill Moyers. *The Power of Myth,* 1988.

2. See Mary Perkins Ryan's reference to the "relaxation of exhaustion," in *Beginning at Home,* 1955, p. 112.

3. See *The Relaxation and Stress Reduction Workbook,* available from New Harbinger Publications, Oakland, CA.

4. This gatha is the subject of a Dharma session reported in Nhat Hanh. *Blooming op. cit.,* as well as in the videocassette, "Practicing Peace," to which reference has already been made.

5. See David Ison's "The Musical Body," to which reference has already been made.

6. This deep wellspring of relaxation is the physical/mental basis for the remarkable injunction to practice "observing the body in the body," etc., which appears in *Transformation and Healing,* Nhat Hanh's translation of and commentary on Buddha's Sutra of the Four Foundations of Mindfulness.

7. See Note 14, Endnotes for Chapter 2.

8. See Note 11, Endnotes for Chapter 2.

Exercise Two

1. Thich Nhat Hanh. *The Miracle of Mindfulness,* 1975.

2. *Ibid.,* p. 15.

3. William Johnson (ed.). *The Cloud of Unknowing,* 1973, p. 56.

Exercise Four

1. See Note 35, Chapter 2.

2. See Note 4, Chapter 3, Exercise One.

3. S. Suzuki. *op. cit.,* p. 32.

4. In Thomas Del Prete. *Thomas Merton and the Education of the Whole Person,* 1990, p. 44f.

5. In the section, "The Three Metamorphoses." *The Portable Nietzsche,* edited and translated by Walter Kaufman, 1954, p.139.
6. Karl Rahner. "How to Receive a Sacrament and Really Mean It." *Theological Digest,* Vol. 19, No. 3 (Autumn 1971), p. 97.
7. Teresa of Avila. "The Interior Castle" quoted in *Light from Light, an Anthology of Christian Mysticism,* edited by Louis Dupré & James A. Wiseman OSB, 1988, p. 271.
8. Rinpoche. *op. cit.,* p. 65.

Exercise Five

1. See Note 6, Chapter 3, Exercise Two.
2. Thomas Merton. "The General Dance." *New Seeds of Contemplation,* 1961, p. 297.
3. Nhat Hanh. *Miracle op. cit.,* p. 30.

Exercise Seven

1. Keating, Pennington and Clark. *op. cit.,* pp. 12-18.
2. Farid al-Din 'Attar in Catherine Hughes (ed.). *The Secret Shrine (Islamic Mystical Reflections),* 1974, [unpaginated]

Exercise Ten

1. Nhat Hanh. *Miracle op. cit.,* p. 58.
2. See Note 37, Chapter 1.

Index

D

E

F

G

H

I

J

K

L

M

Mac/Mc

N

O

P

Q

R

S

T

V

W

Y

Z